100 THINGS
NOTRE DAME FANS
SHOULD KNOW & DO
BEFORE THEY DIE

John Heisler

TRIUMPH
BOOKS

Triumph Books and colophon are registered trademarks of Random House, Inc.

Library of Congress Cataloging-in-Publication Data

Heisler, John.
 100 things Notre Dame fans should know & do before they die / John Heisler.
    p. cm.
 Includes bibliographical references.
 ISBN 978-1-60078-254-1
  1. University of Notre Dame—Football—History—Miscellanea.
 2. Notre Dame Fighting Irish (Football team)—History—Miscellanea.
 I. Title. II. Title: One hundred things Notre Dame fans should know & do before they die.
  GV958.N6H42 2009
  796.332'630977289—dc22

                                                        2009011379

This book is available in quantity at special discounts for your group or organization. For further information, contact:
    Triumph Books
    542 South Dearborn Street
    Suite 750
    Chicago, Illinois 60605
    (312) 939-3330
    Fax (312) 663-3557
    www.triumphbooks.com

Printed in U.S.A.
ISBN: 978-1-60078-254-1
Design by Patricia Frey
All photos courtesy of the University of Notre Dame unless otherwise indicated

For Notre Dame fans everywhere

Contents

Foreword

When I think back to the time that I first began to consider attending the University of Notre Dame, it seems like just yesterday.

Lou Holtz's 1988 football team won the national championship when I was a junior in high school in the Chicago area. The next year, when I was a senior, the Irish ended up 12–1 with a 23-game winning streak that's still a school record. It was hard *not* to hear about Notre Dame football every time you turned around.

When I enrolled in the fall of 1990, it was the continuation of a great period at Notre Dame. In my four seasons, we won a combined 40 games, including victories in the Sugar Bowl and Cotton Bowl (two years in a row) my last three seasons. In three of those seasons, we finished sixth or better in the final polls. We had a lot of great players, and it was great fun.

When the San Francisco 49ers drafted me in the spring of 1994, I had a chance to play for another franchise with great tradition. We won the Super Bowl that very first season, and the 14 years I spent there were tremendous. All things considered, I couldn't have asked for more out of my football career.

Once I decided to retire after the 2007 season, I took some time with my family to decide where to go next. I wasn't sure yet if I wanted to coach either at the collegiate or professional level. I considered the possibility of the administrative end of football, as well. We talked about it as a family, and we prayed on it, too.

But I always kept coming back to Notre Dame. I thought about all the things that were part of my experience here. I thought about all the things I'd learned while being around the game of football all these years. And I decided that becoming part of the Notre Dame staff, even breaking in on the ground level with Charlie Weis and the rest of his coaches, was what I really wanted to do. I know I'm going to learn a lot in the process, and I hope I can pass along some of the things I've learned along the way to the players at Notre Dame.

What led me back to Notre Dame? You'll understand when you flip through the chapters of *100 Things Notre Dame Fans Should Know & Do Before They Die*.

All of those memorable aspects about Notre Dame football haven't changed much in the 20 years or so since I came to school in South Bend. Some of them are the history and tradition that we've all heard about—the Four Horsemen and "Win One for the Gipper" and all that. Some of them include the Heisman Trophy winners and all the great players and teams that are the heritage of football at Notre Dame. Some of them surround the culture of Notre Dame football—the helmets, the Golden Dome, the tunnel at Notre Dame Stadium, and so much more.

That's probably what excites me the most about the 2009 season—I have a chance to be part of all of that again. It's kind of a throwback experience for me on a personal basis, and I can't adequately describe exactly what it means to be at Notre Dame once again.

Without question, part of the explanation is within the stories you'll read in the coming pages—in the games and the players and the coaches and the teams themselves. All the elements of Notre Dame football that make it something special shine just as brightly for me today as they did two decades ago when I enrolled. I'm guessing they'll still be shining two decades from now. (By then, maybe I'll be ready to retire from coaching!)

So sit back and enjoy *100 Things Notre Dame Fans Should Know & Do Before They Die*. It's a perfect read for anyone who wants to gain more of an appreciation for why people like me feel the way we do about football at the University of Notre Dame.

—Bryant Young, University of Notre Dame graduate assistant football coach
1993 team captain and All-American
1994 University of Notre Dame graduate

Introduction

Actually, the first part of the assignment didn't seem so daunting:

Pick the 100 things you need to know about or do if you really want to say you are a University of Notre Dame football fan.

Irish history and tradition have supplied plenty of raw material for that one, including national championships (lots of them), Heisman Trophy winners (seven), All-Americans (lots of those, too), Hall of Fame coaches, plus all kinds of great games and great seasons.

Package all of that into the most legendary on-campus football stadium in America—and throw in all the bells and whistles that go along with a football weekend at Notre Dame—and you've gone a long way to filling out that list.

Okay, okay—so how tough was it to come up with Rockne and Gipp and the Four Horsemen and the 1966 Notre Dame–Michigan State game and all the other obvious moments in Irish lore?

But then came the hardest part.

I went back and reread the email. It said the 100 items should be "ranked in order of importance from 1–100."

Gulp.

So I thought about this part of the assignment for a while, and I decided it wouldn't be too hard to find a good number of the items that deserved to be highly rated. Many were rather obvious, though I'm still not sure how you decide whether a game outrates a season, or whether an All-Star player outpolls a legendary coach.

I gulped again. Then I had an idea.

I asked my wife, Karen, who knows more after having lived 30 years of it firsthand than most people about Notre Dame football. Normally, she is in a proofreading mode for a project like this, so this request came off a bit bolder.

I handed her the tentative list of items—at that point in no particular order—and explained what needed to be done. She looked at the two-page single-spaced list, thought about it for a bit, and finally said, "That's impossible."

So I said, "Now, wait a minute. You can't take a defeatist attitude about this. There is no right or wrong. Everybody has a right to their own opinion. That's the fun of this. You can argue about this all day long."

Somewhat grudgingly, she went back to the list, took her time and went through it, and scribbled some numbers next to her top 20 items or so. And some of that is reflected in what you will see on these pages.

Is this list perfect? Is it even sanctioned? I'm afraid not.

You may have been following football at Notre Dame for 50 years—or for 50 minutes—and either way, there's no chance your list would be the same as this one. No problem.

Maybe the hardest part was all the peripheral elements connected to Fighting Irish football—many of them from the color-and-pageantry department.

The "Play Like A Champion" sign in the passageway that leads from the Notre Dame locker room to the tunnel and the Notre Dame Stadium field has become one of the most photographed spots anywhere on campus (based on access). But where should it rate in comparison with hard-core football events and people?

Pep rallies over time developed into integral parts of a Notre Dame football weekend, compared to the old days when they were mainly student-only affairs.

Tim McCarthy, formerly of the Indiana State Police, still delivers his weekly safety zinger at home games. He's become something of an institution—and now more people even know what he looks like!

Rudy (actually Dan Ruettiger)—both the person and the movie—have helped identify Notre Dame and Irish football for a whole generation of fans, many of whom have never been to South

Bend and have formed much of their opinion about Notre Dame from that film.

And where to put the sign or McCarthy or Rudy on that list? Phew!

Let's just say, when it came to many of the passages, especially on the back end of the list, we simply threw them into a hat and pulled them out. No reason to lose any sleep trying to figure out why your favorite player didn't rate as highly as you might have liked—or why a particular game ended up lower than you would have listed it. That's not what this is all about.

What we really have is a celebration of everything Notre Dame football.

There are dozens more players, many of All-America caliber, with great stories to tell. We barely scratched the surface of game stories worth recounting. Maybe that means there's room for volumes two and three.

And, for the dyed-in-the-wool fan that has already read every word printed on paper or in cyberspace on the subject of Irish football, we at least hope we've provided a few odds and ends of trivia and fact that you didn't know about.

More than anything, consider this book as some sort of stab at a primer on Notre Dame football. You may not be able to name the third-string, right-side linebacker on the 1978 team (that would be Bob Crable, then a freshman, and later a two-time, first-team All-American), but if you become conversant about these 100 items in Irish lore, you're off to a great start. Want to know more about those third-string guys? Volumes two and three may be right up your alley.

In the meantime, the next time you meet someone who just saw *Rudy* for the first time and wants to know more about Notre Dame football, let them borrow your copy of *100 Things Notre Dame Fans Should Know & Do Before They Die*.

You will have done your part to spread the gospel that is football at Notre Dame.

1 Knute Rockne

He Could Coach—And So Much More

Knute Rockne first put his personal stamp on the Notre Dame football program back in 1913 when, as a senior end on the Irish roster, he collaborated with quarterback Gus Dorais to help beat powerful Army in a game that firmly attached Notre Dame's name to the college football map. But it was five years later, when he became the Irish head football coach in 1918, that he began a 13-year tour of duty that saw his star rise to the highest point in the Notre Dame galaxy.

In those 13 seasons, Rockne produced five Notre Dame teams that finished unbeaten and untied, plus six more with only a single loss. His Notre Dame squads produced consensus national titles in 1924, 1929, and 1930. He won 105 games against only 12 defeats—and his all-time winning percentage of .881 remains the best in the history of college football.

Along the way, Rockne coached legendary figures like the Four Horsemen and all-around superstar George Gipp. On 11 occasions, Rockne's players were selected as consensus All-Americans—and eight Notre Dame players that he coached are now in the College Football Hall of Fame.

Originally hired as a chemistry research assistant, Rockne was also a master motivator and marketer whose flair for promotion and the creation of national rivalries against teams like USC furthered the Notre Dame football name.

He also served as Notre Dame's athletics director, business manager, ticket distributor, and track coach. He authored three

*Coach Knute Rockne stands in front of his top-of-the-line 1929 Studebaker
President model FH Victoria on the 125" wheelbase. Rockne was a spokesperson
for the South Bend–based auto manufacturer from 1929 until his death in 1931.*

books, helped design Notre Dame Stadium, opened a stock brokerage firm in South Bend, and was a spokesman for Studebaker.

When the College Football Hall of Fame inducted its first class
in 1951, one of the names on the list was Knute Rockne. That came
20 years after Rockne died tragically in a plane crash near Bazaar,
Kansas.

Actually, Rockne had a rude introduction to football.

As a young Norwegian immigrant to the Logan Square district
of Chicago, Rockne first played the game with his immigrant
neighbors on the sandlots. A slender and swift ball carrier, Rockne
broke away from his pursuers for a long run, a sure touchdown. But
a rowdy group of fans for the opponents stepped in, stripped the
ball away from his cradled arms, and mistook his body for a punch-
ing bag.

When Rockne finally arrived home, his parents took one look at his tattered body and announced that his football career was over. But a few bumps and bruises would not keep Rockne away from the game he loved for long. With his parents' blessing, he returned to the gridiron in high school and later emerged as the country's most respected, innovative, and successful college football coach of all time.

After Rockne finished high school, he worked as a mail dispatcher with the Chicago Post Office for four years and continued his athletic endeavors at the Irving Park Athletic Club, the Central YMCA, and the Illinois Athletic Club. By then he had saved enough money to continue his education and boarded the train for South Bend and Notre Dame. After a difficult first year as a scrub with the varsity, Rockne turned his attention to track where he earned a monogram and later set a school record (12–4) in the indoor pole vault. Those accomplishments gave him incentive to give football another try. This time he succeeded and eventually was named to Walter Camp's All-America football squad as a third-string end. During his senior season (1913) when he served as captain, Rockne and his roommate, quarterback Gus Dorais, stunned Army with their deadly pass combination and handed the high-ranking Cadets a 35–13 setback.

But Rockne—who also fought semi-professionally in South Bend, wrote for the student newspaper and yearbook, played flute in the school orchestra, took a major role in every student play, and reached the finals of the Notre Dame marbles tournament—considered himself primarily a student. He worked his way through school, first as a janitor and then as a chemistry research assistant to Professor Julius A. Nieuwland, whose discoveries led to synthetic rubber. Rockne graduated magna cum laude with a 90.52 (on a scale of 100) grade average.

Upon graduation, Rockne was offered a post at Notre Dame as a graduate assistant in chemistry. He accepted that position on the condition that he be allowed to help Jesse Harper coach the football team. When Harper retired after the 1917 season, Rockne was named his successor.

Under Rockne's tutelage, Notre Dame skyrocketed to national prominence and became America's team. With their penchant for upsetting the stronger, more established football powers throughout the land, the Irish captured the hearts of millions of Americans who viewed Notre Dame's victories as hope for their own battles.

"The old padre running the University understood marketing. He realized that up the road in Chicago there was a newspaper or two he could use," said longtime ABC Sports college play-by-play veteran Keith Jackson.

"They were in the perfect position to capitalize because they were a private university. You have to remember, they were called the Catholics for a while. The circumstances were just right. They had a coach and an athletic director in Jess Harper who could deliver.

"Then Knute Rockne came along. He was a chemistry teacher and he might have gone to Alaska and sold refrigerators if he hadn't gone into football. He was a salesman, and he could have sold anything. Notre Dame had Chicago and New York. Columbia never captured New York City. Notre Dame has always been the dominant college football team in New York City because there are all kinds of Catholics there. Not just the Irish."

During Rockne's 13-year coaching tenure, Notre Dame beat Stanford in the 1925 Rose Bowl and put together five unbeaten and untied seasons. Rockne produced 20 first-team All-Americans. His lifetime winning percentage of .881 (105–12–5) still ranks at the top of the list for both college and professional football. Rockne won the last 19 games he coached. Rockne, who was inducted into the National Football Foundation Hall of Fame in 1951—the first year of inductions—revolutionized the game of football with his wide-ranging ideas and innovations. Rockne was the first football coach to take his team all over the country and initiate intersectional rivalries. The Irish competed in a national arena. He challenged the best football teams in the land and almost always won.

For all of his contributions to the game of football, *The Sporting News* recognized Rockne as the 76th most powerful person in sports for the twentieth century. In its 2008 book, *The College Football Book*, *Sports Illustrated* listed Rockne and Alabama's Bear Bryant as its all-time coaches.

The *NCAA Official Football Records Book* listed 12 major college dynasties from the twentieth century "because of historical significance, and all represent an outstanding record as well as at least one national championship." Notre Dame was one of three schools to place two dynasties on that list (1919–30 under Rockne; 1946–53 under Frank Leahy), with Oklahoma (1948–58; 1971–80) and Alabama (1959–67; 1971–80) also earning double distinction.

Using his medical and anatomical knowledge, Rockne designed his own equipment and uniforms. He reduced the amount of bulk and weight of the equipment, while increasing its protectiveness. He also introduced the gold satin and silk pants that cut down on wind resistance. Rockne foresaw the day of the two-platoon system and often used his "shock troops," a full team of second-stringers, at the start of most games.

Inspired by the precision and timing of a chorus line, Rockne added the Notre Dame shift to his playbook. In the shift, all four backs were still in motion at the snap. Opponents were so dumbfounded by the shift that they couldn't find a consistent way to handle it. The rules board finally enacted a law against the shift. Rockne also attempted to outsmart his coaching peers by downplaying his squads' talent. He never boasted about his team or its strengths; rather, he lamented his squad's lack of skill every chance he got. Rockne believed that half of football strategy was passing, while most of his counterparts kept the ball on the ground.

"Rockne is the greatest college football figure of the twentieth century, no ifs, ands, buts about it," said ESPN's Beano Cook. "People recognize his picture now. They know it's Rockne. When he died, if I recall, it was the first funeral ever broadcast nationally on radio. That's the kind of impact he had. For me, it was easy to pick Rockne as the No. 1 coach. He has been dead 70 years, and everybody still knows his name."

But football was never enough for Rockne. He also served as Notre Dame's athletic director, business manager, ticket distributor, track coach, and equipment manager; he wrote a newspaper column once a week; he authored three books, including a volume of juvenile fiction; he was principle designer of Notre Dame Stadium; he opened a stock brokerage firm in South Bend during his last season; he was a dedicated family man to his wife Bonnie and their four children and for years raised much of the family's food in his garden. Rockne also made several public speeches a year and served as a public spokesman for Studebaker.

After the championship season of 1930, Rockne tried to get away for a much-needed rest and vacation. But he was needed in Los Angeles to make a football demonstration movie.

An enthusiastic flier and never one to waste time, Rockne boarded Transcontinental-Western's Flight 599 from Kansas City to Los Angeles on March 31, 1931. Shortly after takeoff, the plane flew into a storm, became covered with ice, and fell into a wheat field near Bazaar, Kansas. There were no survivors.

Rockne became the first athletic coach at any level to be featured on a United States postage stamp on March 9, 1988, when a commemorative stamp in his honor was dedicated at Notre Dame. The stamp honored the 100th anniversary of Rockne's birth. Approximately 160 million Rockne stamps were printed, with the first-day issue originating from the University of Notre Dame Post Office. Highlighting the unveiling of the stamp was an appearance and speech at the Joyce Center by President Ronald Reagan, who played George Gipp in the 1940 Warner Brothers movie *Knute Rockne, All-American.*

2 Revisit Old Notre Dame Stadium

Legendary History for Irish Grid Facility

For all the legendary players and memorable moments it has hosted on its bluegrass turf over the past 405 games (through 2008), Notre Dame Stadium has unquestionably developed a lore all its own. In service to Irish football since 1930, the stadium continues to be one of the most recognizable and revered structures in the world of sports.

But the Notre Dame Stadium that Irish fans have visited and viewed since 1997 underwent the most involved expansion and remodeling since the facility was first built. More than 21,000 new seats are now available, bringing capacity to 80,795.

It was the success of Knute Rockne's Notre Dame football teams—plus the legendary coach's own personal building blueprint—that prompted the addition of the original Notre Dame Stadium to the University's athletic plant back in 1930.

The spirit that was imbued by the Rockne era—and has been sustained by seven Heisman Trophy winners and dozens more All-Americans who have competed on that turf—has changed little in more than seven decades of football at Notre Dame Stadium.

The Irish first played their games on Cartier Field, then located just north of the current stadium site. As the University's national football reputation expanded, thanks to Rockne's coaching, the need for a new home for the Irish was voiced because no more than 30,000 fans could squeeze into the Cartier facility.

An arial view of Notre Dame Stadium on its dedication day, October 11, 1930. The Irish defeated traditional foe Navy, 26–2.

Architectural blueprints and bids were received from prominent contractors throughout the nation once plans became more specific by 1929. The Osborn Engineering Company, which had designed more than 50 stadia in the country—including Comiskey Park in Chicago, Yankee Stadium and the Polo Grounds in New York City, and facilities at Michigan, Indiana, Purdue, and Minnesota—was awarded the contract, and excavation began that summer.

Actual labor on the foundations of the Stadium did not commence until April 1930, but four months later Notre Dame Stadium opened its 18 gates for its first use.

The Stadium measured a half-mile in circumference, stood 45 feet high, and featured a glass-enclosed press box rising 60 feet above ground level. It originally accommodated 264 writers plus facilities for photographers and radio and television broadcasters. There were more than 2,000,000 bricks in the original edifice, 400 tons of steel, and 15,000 cubic yards of concrete. The cost of construction exceeded $750,000. Architecturally, the Notre Dame Stadium was patterned on a smaller scale after the University of Michigan's mammoth stadium.

Though Rockne had a chance to coach in the new facility only in its initial season of use, he took a personal hand in its design. The sod from Cartier Field was transplanted into the new Stadium, but Rockne insisted on its use for football only. He kept the area between the field and the stands small to keep sideline guests, as he called them, to a minimum—and he personally supervised the parking and traffic system that remained much the same until the 21,150-seat addition in 1997.

With a crowd on hand far less than the 54,000 capacity, the Irish opened the facility by defeating SMU 20–14 on October 4, 1930. Official dedication ceremonies came a week later against traditional foe Navy. This time, more than 40,000 fans cheered a 26–2 triumph over the Midshipmen. Frank E. Hering, captain of the 1898 team and the first Notre Dame coach as well as president of the Alumni Association, delivered the major speech during the ceremonies.

It took another year before the Irish played before their first capacity crowd (50,731 for the 1931 USC game), but full houses and Notre Dame victories have been the rule rather than the exception. Since that 1930 opening, the Irish have compiled an impressive 302–98–5 (.751) mark in Notre Dame Stadium (through 2008), while an average of 62,463 spectators have watched.

During 25 of those seasons, the Irish did not lose at home. Beginning with a 27–20 win over Northwestern on November 21, 1942, and ending with a 28–14 loss to Purdue on October 7, 1950, Notre Dame won 28 straight games in Notre Dame Stadium. The

Irish went 6–0 at home in 1998, their most recent undefeated season at home and their first since 1989.

Notre Dame's largest crowd ever to witness a game in the Stadium prior to the expansion was 61,296 in a 24–6 loss to Purdue on October 6, 1962. However, attendance figures since 1966 have been based on paid admissions, rather than total in the house, thus accounting for the familiar 59,075 figure every week prior to 1997.

Since that 1966 season, every Irish home game has been a sellout with the exception of a Thanksgiving Day matchup with Air Force in 1973. That game, won by the Irish 48–15, was changed to the holiday to accommodate national television and was played with students absent from campus.

Navy again was the opponent in 1979 when Notre Dame celebrated the 50th season of service of Notre Dame Stadium. Commemorative-edition tickets, which were authentic reproductions used for the 1930 dedication game, were used.

The final home game of 1991 against Tennessee saw two more stadium milestones reached. The 100th straight sellout crowd entered the stadium, which was hosting its 300th game since the 1930 opening.

The 2008 season featured two more milestones. The season opener against San Diego State marked the 200th consecutive sellout at Notre Dame Stadium—and the victory a week later versus Michigan marked Notre Dame's 300th win in the Stadium.

Overall, 316 of the 405 games (including 253 of the last 254 through 2008) played in Notre Dame Stadium have been viewed by capacity crowds for a .780 percentage.

Sports Illustrated compiled a list of its favorite sports venues of the twentieth century, with the top five including Yankee Stadium, Augusta National Golf Club, Army's Michie Stadium, Duke's Cameron Indoor Stadium, and the Bislett Stadium skating oval in Oslo, Norway.

In addition to Michie, the only other college football facility in the top 20 was Notre Dame Stadium (No. 18), with the magazine proclaiming, "Touchdown Jesus keeps an eye on one end zone, and Knute Rockne watches over the rest of the field. Rockne built his dream stadium and coached here in 1930, its first season, his last." In 2001, *The Sporting News* listed Notre Dame Stadium second on its list of top 10 college football cathedrals in America.

Another recent article, by Wendell Barnhouse in the *Fort Worth Star-Telegram* (September 2002), listed Notre Dame Stadium as having the third-best game atmosphere of any college facility in the country, trailing only Texas A&M's Kyle Field and Florida's Ben Hill Griffin Stadium. Here's some of what Barnhouse had to say about Notre Dame Stadium:

"Attend a game in South Bend on an early fall afternoon, and you feel the history, the tradition, and the legends washing over you like a waterfall. From the Grotto to Touchdown Jesus to the Golden Dome to the statue of Frank Leahy to the stadium itself, it's a place where goosebumps break out with every step and each breath.... More history has been written in this stadium than any other. Notre Dame Stadium has been home to seven Heisman Trophy winners and eight of the program's 11 national champions. The phrase 'Shake Down The Thunder' is more appropriate than ever when a full house roars its approval as the Fighting Irish take the field. Notre Dame Stadium is a simple stadium, with its rows of seats descending to the edge of the playing field. And when Notre Dame plays another traditional power, such as Michigan or Nebraska, the goosebumps multiply.... Rockne, the Gipper, Touchdown Jesus, Friday night pep rallies, the leprechaun, the tailgaters. You can read about college football history, or you can just go to a game here."

Finally, in the September 20, 1996, edition of the *Los Angeles Times*, writer Chris Dufresne called Notre Dame the best place to watch a college football game, writing, "If it's fall, and the leaves are turning, and Notre Dame is winning, you set it to music."

Lou Holtz

The Great Motivator

Lou Holtz's first season as head coach at Notre Dame in 1986 saw the Irish lose five games by a combined total of 14 points. The next year, the Irish won eight games and played in the Cotton Bowl. The following season, Holtz's Irish won 12 games and the national title—and 20 years after that championship season, Holtz was inducted into the College Football Hall of Fame in 2008.

Holtz coached 11 seasons at Notre Dame and guided his teams to 100 wins—second only to Knute Rockne in total victories. He remains eighth (through 2008) on the NCAA all-time win list for Division I-A coaches (with 249). Holtz took his Notre Dame teams to nine straight New Year's Day bowl games from 1987 through '95 and coached the Irish to finishes of sixth or better in the final Associated Press poll in five seasons.

Holtz was named the national coach of the year in 1988 and saw his team play the most difficult schedule in the country three different years. His teams won 32 games against teams ranked in the AP top 25 during his career with the Irish, and Notre Dame also won a record 23 straight games in 1988 and '89.

He coached 19 first-team Irish All-Americans, a Heisman Trophy winner in Tim Brown, two Lombardi winners in Chris Zorich and Aaron Taylor, a Walter Camp Player of the Year in Raghib Ismail, and a Johnny Unitas winner in Tony Rice.

The Kent State graduate also coached at William & Mary, North Carolina State, Arkansas, Minnesota, and South Carolina— and then joined ESPN as a studio analyst.

In 33 seasons as a college head coach, Holtz compiled 249 wins and took a record six different programs to bowl games. He

"You're never as good as everyone tells you when you win, and you're never as bad as they say when you lose." Coach Lou Holtz knew a thing or two about winning—he guided Notre Dame to 100 wins in his 11 seasons.

saw 23 of his teams qualify for bowl games and 18 finish in the final AP top 25.

In 2008, Holtz received the Moose Krause Man of the Year award from the Notre Dame Monogram Club for his off-the-field contributions.

A sculpture of Holtz was dedicated on September 13, 2008, at Notre Dame Stadium's Gate D, which honors the Irish national championship football coaches. Speaking at the dedication on behalf of Holtz's former players was 1987 Heisman Trophy winner

Tim Brown. Other speakers included *New York Times* best-selling author Harvey Mackay, Notre Dame president Rev. John I. Jenkins, C.S.C., and Notre Dame athletics director Jack Swarbrick. Assisting with the sculpture unveiling were former Holtz players Chris Zorich, Pat Terrell, and Ned Bolcar, all members of the 1988 Irish national championship squad.

The Holtz sculpture shows the former Irish coach calling a play on the sidelines, with two Irish players (Tim Brown and Skip Holtz were the models) beside him. Notre Dame graduate Jerry McKenna created the sculpture. He also created the Frank Leahy and Moose Krause sculpture east of Notre Dame Stadium, the Knute Rockne sculpture at the College Football Hall of Fame in downtown South Bend, Indiana, and the Ara Parseghian sculpture that was dedicated in 2007 at the same Notre Dame Stadium Gate D location. The sculpture was funded by donations from Holtz's former players, assistant coaches, student managers, friends, and business associates.

The sculpture complements bas relief portraits of the five Notre Dame national championship coaches—Rockne, Leahy, Parseghian, Dan Devine, and Holtz—that are located at Gate D, designated the national championship coaches gate.

4 Ara Parseghian

Could He *Really* Stop the Rain?

When Ara Parseghian came from Northwestern to take over Notre Dame football in December 1963, the Irish program was at a low ebb. Notre Dame had finished 2–7 the previous season and hadn't enjoyed a winning record since 1958.

It didn't take Ara long to change all that. His Irish went on the road and romped past Wisconsin 31–7 to open the 1964 season. They won nine straight games and rose to the No. 1 ranking before falling in the final two minutes at USC to end the season. The National Football Foundation awarded Notre Dame the MacArthur Bowl as its national champion, previously unheralded quarterback John Huarte won the Heisman Trophy, and Parseghian was named the national college coach of the year. Parseghian had put the Irish back into the national spotlight and they never left it during his 11 seasons as head coach in South Bend.

Two years later in 1966, the Irish claimed their eighth consensus national title, rebounding from their epic 10–10 tie with No. 2 Michigan State to vanquish USC 51–0 the following Saturday.

Notre Dame followed that up with a perfect 11–0 campaign and yet another championship banner in 1973, spring-boarded by a midseason victory over sixth-rated USC.

Parseghian's tenure was keynoted by the University's decision to return to postseason bowl competition. That allowed Notre Dame to defeat top-rated and unbeaten Texas in the Cotton Bowl following the 1970 season, then to knock off unbeaten Bear Bryant–coached Alabama teams in the Sugar and Orange Bowls following the 1973 and '74 seasons.

Parseghian won 95 games in his 11 seasons with the Irish, only once losing as many as three games in a year, and his teams finished in the Associated Press top 10 in nine of those 11 years.

In addition to Huarte, Parseghian coached a Maxwell Award winner in Jim Lynch in 1966 and a Lombardi Award winner in Walt Patulski in 1971. He coached 21 consensus All-Americans, including Huarte, Lynch, and Alan Page, all of whom have been selected to the College Football Hall of Fame. In addition, Parseghian had 17 players earn first-team Academic All-America honors and eight winners of NCAA Post-Graduate Scholarships.

"A good coach will make his players see what they can be rather than what they are." In 11 seasons, Ara Parseghian's teams won 95 games, and he coached 21 consensus All-Americans.

Eighty-three of his players were NFL draft picks after his 11 seasons, including a dozen first-round selections.

In 1980, Parseghian was selected to the College Football Hall of Fame.

A sculpture of Parseghian was dedicated on September 22, 2007, at Notre Dame Stadium. More than 200 of his former players attended the dedication—and Huarte spoke on behalf of that group.

The Parseghian sculpture shows the former Irish coach on the shoulders of his players following the 1971 Cotton Bowl win over top-rated Texas. The statue was sculpted by Notre Dame graduate Jerry McKenna, who had previously created the Frank Leahy and Moose Krause statues east of Notre Dame Stadium, as well as the

Knute Rockne sculpture at the College Football Hall of Fame in downtown South Bend, Indiana.

The sculpture was funded completely by donations from Parseghian's former players, assistant coaches, and student managers. Plans for the statue were spearheaded by former Irish football player Peter Schivarelli, who played in 1969–70.

Parseghian previously had been head coach at Northwestern for eight seasons and Miami of Ohio for five before coming to Notre Dame. A fan favorite of the Notre Dame student body, Parseghian at one wet Irish home game heard the students exhort him, "Ara, stop the rain."

In 1994, Parseghian started the Ara Parseghian Medical Research Foundation to fund study of Niemann-Pick Type C Disease in hopes of moving toward a cure. The foundation has raised more than $22 million to combat the disease, which has claimed three of Parseghian's grandchildren. The disease, also known as NP-C, is a genetic pediatric neurodegenerative disorder that causes progressive deterioration of the nervous system, usually in school-aged children. By interfering with children's ability to metabolize cholesterol, NP-C causes large amounts of the substance to accumulate in the liver, spleen, and brain, leading to a series of ultimately fatal neurological problems.

5 George Gipp

Maybe the Best of All Time

George Gipp never won a Heisman Trophy. The Doak Walker Award was decades in the distance. There was no ESPN awards show in his day to feature his achievements.

Still, Gipp was quite possibly the best all-round player in college football history. He presumably would have become a legend even if he had overcome the streptococci throat infection that led to his untimely death at the age of 25.

Ironically, his death on December 14, 1920—coming just two weeks after he was selected by Walter Camp as Notre Dame's first All-American—assured Gipp's place in Notre Dame's history books.

While on his deathbed, Gipp, who had contracted strep throat while helping the Irish defeat Northwestern late in his senior season, made this often-repeated plea to his coach, Knute Rockne:

"I've got to go, Rock. It's all right. I'm not afraid. Some time, Rock, when the team is up against it, when things are wrong and the breaks are beating the boys—tell them to go in there with all they've got and win just one for the Gipper. I don't know where I'll be then, Rock. But I'll know about it, and I'll be happy."

Rockne waited eight years to relay Gipp's parting request. On November 10, 1928, after losing two of its first six games, an injury-riddled Notre Dame team traveled to Yankee Stadium to face unbeaten Army. According to Francis Wallace of the *New York News*, Rockne made this pregame speech to his underdog Irish.

"The day before he died, George Gipp asked me to wait until the situation seemed hopeless—then ask a Notre Dame team to go out and beat Army for him. This is the day, and you are the team."

Notre Dame won the game 12–6 on a pair of second-half touchdowns. Jack Chevigny scored the first on a one-yard run and, after reaching the end zone, said, "That is one for the Gipper." Football experts who witnessed it said the game was the greatest

One of Notre Dame's most versatile players, George Gipp could run, pass, and punt. His career total of 2,341 rushing yards was a school record that lasted more than 50 years until Jerome Heavens broke it in 1978.

demonstration of inspired football ever played anywhere. Even now, more than 80 years later, every aspiring football player, or anyone facing insurmountable odds, hears the tale of the Gipper.

But Gipp should be remembered for much more than his tragic death and dying wish.

Gipp left his home in Laurium, Michigan, in 1916 and headed to Notre Dame with ambitions of playing baseball. But one fall afternoon Rockne spotted Gipp, who had never played football in high school, drop-kicking the football 60 and 70 yards just for the fun of it. The persuasive coach, sensing Gipp's natural athletic ability, eventually convinced Gipp to go out for the team. Gipp experienced nothing but success on the gridiron.

A four-year member of the varsity team, Gipp proved to be the most versatile player Rockne ever had. He could run, he could pass, and he could punt. Still holder of a handful of Notre Dame records in a variety of categories, Gipp led the Irish in rushing and passing each of his last three seasons (1918, 1919, and 1920). His career mark of 2,341 rushing yards lasted more than 50 years until Jerome Heavens broke it in 1978. Gipp did not allow a pass completion in his territory. Walter Camp named him the outstanding college player in America in 1920. Gipp was voted into the National Football Hall of Fame in 1951.

During Gipp's career, Notre Dame compiled a 27–2–3 record, including a 19–0–1 mark in his last 20 games. With Gipp's help, the Irish outscored their opponents 506 to 97 in those contests. Notre Dame was undefeated in 1919 and 1920, and the Irish were declared Champions of the West.

"The College Game" in 1974 rated Gipp a first-team back in the 1910–1919 period. The *Sports Illustrated* Web site, SI.com, rated Gipp the top Notre Dame athlete of all-time (any sport) in its summer 2008 ratings, calling him "perhaps the most versatile player in college football's storied history." The 2008 *Sports Illustrated* book, *The College Football Book,* listed Gipp as a first-team back for the 1920s on its all-decade teams.

Despite his football achievements, Gipp's first love remained baseball. He played center field for the Irish and had planned to join the Chicago Cubs after graduation.

The role of Gipp was later played by a young actor named Ronald Reagan (the Republican who later became President) along-side Pat O'Brien's Rockne in the movie *Knute Rockne, All-American* that has been called the greatest serious college football movie produced in Hollywood.

6 "Win One for the Gipper"

The 1928 Army Game

Knute Rockne was desperate.

His 1928 team, decimated by injuries, had already lost two of its first six games. Three powerful teams—Army, Carnegie Tech, and USC—loomed on the schedule before the season (the worst in Rockne's illustrious coaching career) would mercifully draw to a close.

Rockne knew that if his Ramblers could upend Army—winner of six straight games—in Yankee Stadium, a losing record could be averted. His critics were claiming he'd lost his touch; the magic was gone. But Rockne knew better. The week of the game he quietly told his neighbor that Notre Dame would beat Army. Rockne had a plan. His team might not be able to win on talent, but Notre Dame would win on emotion and spirit. Rockne would deliver what would later become the most famous pep talk in sports history.

After pregame warm-ups, Rockne huddled his players in the locker room. They laid down on World War I blankets that covered the cold, clammy floor. Rockne waited until the room was silent. He lowered his head before speaking.

He began slowly—telling the team about George Gipp, a Notre Dame player who had died during his senior season eight years ago. Although none of the players had known Gipp personally, each and every one of them had heard of his exploits. They knew Gipp had been the greatest player of his time.

Rockne, who had been at Gipp's bedside, repeated the young athlete's last wish.

"This is the day, and you are that team." With those words, coach Knute Rockne turned around Notre Dame's fortunes in the 1928 game vs. Army.

"I've got to go, Rock. It's all right. I'm not afraid. Some time, Rock, when the team is up against it, when things are wrong and the breaks are beating the boys—tell them to go in there with all they've got and win just one for the Gipper. I don't know where I'll be then, Rock. But I'll know about it, and I'll be happy."

Rockne continued:

"The day before he died, George Gipp asked me to wait until the situation seemed hopeless—then ask a Notre Dame team to go out and beat Army for him. This is the day, and you are the team."

"There was no one in the room that wasn't crying," recalled line coach Ed Healy. "There was a moment of silence, and then all of a sudden those players ran out of the dressing room and almost tore the hinges off the door. They were all ready to kill someone."

Army didn't have a chance.

After falling behind 6–0 in the third period, Notre Dame scored two touchdowns and held off a last-chance rally by the Cadets for a 12–6 win.

Jack Chevigny tied the score at 6–6 with a one-yard plunge. As he picked himself up in the end zone, he jumped up and shouted, "That's one for the Gipper!"

The emotional Chevigny was helping Notre Dame drive toward its final and winning score in the last quarter when he was injured. Rockne was forced to take him out and replace him with Bill Drew. Reserve Johnny O'Brien, a willowy hurdler for the track team, took Johnny Colrick's place at left end.

The Irish were 32 yards from the goal line. Left halfback Butch Niemiec took the ball, looked downfield to O'Brien, and flung a wobbly pass over an Army defender. O'Brien hauled the ball in on the 10-yard line, squeezed past two tacklers, and dove into the end zone for the winning touchdown. O'Brien never became a starter in his career with Notre Dame, but "One-Play" was a legitimate hero to Irish fans.

As O'Brien scored, the Notre Dame bench erupted in whoops and hollers. The injured Chevigny cried on the sidelines, "That's one for the Gipper, too."

Even Rockne showed satisfaction with the play.

"You could see a great big smile on his face," said quarterback Frank Carideo. "He was happy when things created during the week were used to perfection in the ballgame."

But O'Brien's touchdown didn't put the game safely away. Army had another chance with less than two minutes to go. The Cadets drove methodically through the Notre Dame defense, helped by a 55-yard kickoff return by All-American Chris Cagle. Cagle, who had played the entire game, collapsed at the 10-yard line because of exhaustion and had to be carried from the field. Dick Hutchinson took the ball to the four and then to the one. But time ran out before the Cadets could get off another play, and Notre Dame had indeed "won one for the Gipper."

The Sporting News released a list of "Top 10 Moments" in college football (November 13, 1999). The No. 3 moment was the legend of Gipp and the famous speech made by Rockne. The magazine's account read: "'The day before he died [in 1920], George Gipp asked me to wait until the situation seemed hopeless.... Then ask a Notre Dame team to beat Army for him,' said Rockne in 1928. 'This is the day and you are that team.' The Irish beat unbeaten Army, 12–6."

7 The "Notre Dame Victory March"

It Ranks No. 1, Too

The most recognizable collegiate fight song in the nation, the "Notre Dame Victory March," was written in the early 1900s by two brothers who were University of Notre Dame graduates. Michael Shea, a 1905 graduate, composed the music—while his brother, John Shea, who earned degrees in 1906 and 1908, provided the corresponding lyrics. The song was copyrighted in 1908 and a piano version, complete with lyrics, was published that year. Michael, who became a priest in Ossining, New York, collaborated on the project with John, who lived in Holyoke, Massachusetts. The song's public debut came in the winter of 1908 when Michael played it on the organ of the Second Congregational Church in Holyoke.

The "Notre Dame Victory March" later was presented by the Shea brothers to the University, and it first appeared under the copyright of the University of Notre Dame in 1928. The copyright was assigned to the publishing company of Edwin H. Morris and the copyright for the beginning of the song is still in effect. The more well-known second verse, which begins with the words "Cheer, cheer for Old Notre Dame," is now in the public domain in the United States (for both the music and lyrics)—but the second verse remains protected in all territories outside of the country.

Notre Dame's fight song was first performed at Notre Dame on Easter Sunday of 1909 in the rotunda of the Administration Building. The Notre Dame band, under the direction of Professor Clarence Peterson, performed the "Victory March" as part of its traditional Easter morning concert. It was first heard at a Notre Dame athletic event 10 years later.

In 1969, as college football celebrated its centennial, the "Notre Dame Victory March" was honored as the "greatest of all fight songs."

Michael Shea was pastor of St. Augustine's Church in Ossining until his death in 1938. John Shea, a baseball monogram winner at Notre Dame, became a Massachusetts state senator and lived in Holyoke until his death in 1965.

Rally sons of Notre Dame
Sing her glory and sound her fame,
Raise her Gold and Blue
And cheer with voices true:
Rah, rah, for Notre Dame
We will fight in ev-ry game,
Strong of heart and true to her name
We will ne'er forget her
And will cheer her ever
Loyal to Notre Dame

Cheer, cheer for old Notre Dame,
Wake up the echoes cheering her name,
Send a volley cheer on high,
Shake down the thunder from the sky.
What though the odds be great or small
Old Notre Dame will win over all,
While her loyal sons are marching
Onward to victory.

The original lyrics, written when all athletes at Notre Dame were male, refer to "sons," but in recognition of the fact that the "Victory March" is now played for athletic teams composed of men and women, many modify the words accordingly. The "Victory March" earned a No. 1 ranking in ratings compiled in the 1998 book, *College Fight Songs: An Annotated Anthology*. The "Victory March" was also the No. 1-ranked fight song in a survey in 1990 by Bill Studwell, a librarian at Northern Illinois University.

When *Saturday Afternoon* in 1985 rated its "Ten Greatest Things Abut College Football" by ESPN's Beano Cook, in second place after "The Dotting of the I at Ohio State" came "Hearing the 'Victory March' at Notre Dame."

Cook wrote, "When the 'Victory March' starts and the team comes out of the tunnel, it's kind of like hearing the National Anthem when you're in a foreign country. It does something to you. That is, of course, as long as your team isn't the one playing Notre Dame. If you happen to be the visiting team, it's no fun.

"Did you know the 'Victory March' is the fourth most famous song in America? The National Anthem is No. 1, although nobody knows the words to the second verse. Then there's 'God Bless America,' 'White Christmas,' and the 'Victory March.' You have to have Kate Smith sing 'God Bless America,' Bing Crosby singing

'White Christmas,' and you have to be at Notre Dame to appreciate the 'Victory March.'"

The "Victory March" was judged to be the best college fight song by 31 percent of a cnnsi.com Internet poll respondents a few years back (Michigan's fight song was second with 27 percent, followed by the Texas song at 26).

Notre Dame's Band of the Fighting Irish celebrated the 100th anniversary of the "Victory March" during the 2008 football season.

8 Notre Dame Hits the National Map

The 1913 Army Game

When Army reluctantly agreed to pay Notre Dame $1,000 for its long journey to the plains of West Point in 1913, the good-but-stingy generals conceded the hefty sum would be worth a victory. Although the Cadets knew coach Jesse Harper's Irish were a Midwestern powerhouse (they'd lost just one game the previous three seasons), most Army fans felt Notre Dame would serve merely as a tasty appetizer for the West Pointers' annual picnic with Navy. The Irish might be able to give Army a run for its money, but surely the Cadets' gridiron superiority would crush the Hoosier hayseeds who had arrived from their all-day train trip with 18 players—and just 14 pairs of cleats.

Army, which had scouted Notre Dame's 62–0 thrashing of Alma, was expecting a hard-hitting, powerful running attack led by a strong line. Instead, the Cadets found themselves in the middle of an unrelenting blitzkrieg.

Notre Dame got off to a rocky start. After winning the coin toss and electing to receive (a bold move in those days), quarterback Gus Dorais fumbled during the opening series, and Army recovered on the Irish 27-yard line. But the potent Cadet offense gained just one yard on three tries, and the Army began to realize that $1,000 was a steep price tag for humiliation.

Notre Dame's surprising passing game helped the visitors stake claim to a 14–13 lead at halftime. The Cadets certainly weren't strangers to the aerial toss; in fact, Army was the premier passing team of the East. But the Cadets, along with the rest of the football world, thought passes were thrown only in desperation—as a last resort. The West Pointers couldn't adjust to a team using the pass as its bread and butter.

So the Irish offense continued to shoot rockets in the second half, and Army, with a young cadet named Dwight Eisenhower sitting on the bench, failed miserably on defense.

When Dorais wasn't hurling spirals to Knute Rockne (a technique the pair had mastered during the summer when they worked as lifeguards at the beach resort of Cedar Point, Ohio, where a plaque pays tribute to their summer workouts), Ray Eichenlaub would break through the line for a long gain. Even the Army partisans oohed and aahed at Notre Dame's amazing versatility.

Years later, in a 1930 *Collier's Weekly* edition, Rockne wrote, "We spent a whole summer vacation in 1913 at Cedar Point on Lake Erie. We worked our way as restaurant checkers, but played our way on the beach with a football, practicing the forward pass. There was nothing much else for two young fellows without much pocket money to do, and it made us familiar with the innovation that was to change the entire character of football."

By game's end, Dorais had completed 14-of-17 passes (he misfired on his first two tries) for 243 yards—unheard of totals in

1913. And his 40-yard toss to Rockne was the longest pass ever completed to that day. Notre Dame had rocked the football world with its stunning 35–13 victory.

The win revolutionized college football as the forward pass, a legal weapon since 1906, gained popularity as a legitimate offensive tool.

"The press and the football public hailed this new game, and Notre Dame received credit as the originator of a style of play that we simply systematized," Rockne said.

Notre Dame also earned a national reputation with its victory, and teams from all over the East were clamoring for a matchup.

Notre Dame had made it to the big time, appearing on *Sports Illustrated's* list of the century's greatest games (in all sports), with its 35–13 victory over Army in that November 1, 1913, game checking in at No. 11.

"Of all the echoes bouncing around South Bend, this one reverberates loudest. It wasn't just that the unknown Irish whipped the undefeated Cadet juggernaut, it was how they did it—with what had heretofore been a gimmick, the forward pass. Notre Dame's Gus Dorais went 14-for-17 for 243 yards and two touchdowns, one to halfback Joe Pliska, the other to Knute Rockne. Army was so bewitched, bothered, and bewildered by the aerial antics that it surely didn't even matter that one of their halfbacks, Dwight David Eisenhower, was out with an injury."

The top spot belonged to the 1982 NFL playoff game between San Diego and Miami. The only other college football games on this top 20 list were the 1984 Boston College–Miami game (No. 3) and the 1982 California-Stanford matchup (No. 20).

9 Walk Out the Notre Dame Stadium Tunnel

One of the Unique Experiences in all of College Football

Former Notre Dame All-American offense lineman Aaron Taylor said it best.

"I was fortunate to have a career in professional football and I played in two Super Bowls and we won one of them. But it still doesn't compare to the thrill of running out of the tunnel in Notre Dame Stadium."

These days, there's at least something to identify the space as Notre Dame's. A few years back, the Notre Dame Monogram Club

The trip through the tunnel at Notre Dame Stadium is one of the most exhilarating moments in college football.

added banners for each of Notre Dame's national championship seasons. They're attached to the cement ceiling and in full view as you take the field. But for years, the area was as nondescript as many other elements of Notre Dame football.

Until the remodeling of the area during the 1996–97 renovation, both teams came into the tunnel down single-file stairs from their respective locker rooms. The quarters were so close that security officials had to make sure to separate the two groups since they generally were assigned by television to come onto the field one after another and there was little room for fraternization.

The tunnel is 23 feet wide, and the ceiling above it just 18 feet high at the base of the slight sloped runway. Notre Dame players file past the "Play Like A Champion Today" sign just before entering the tunnel area.

Joe Montana

The Comeback Kid

Joe Montana never officially earned All-America honors at Notre Dame. And his name isn't necessarily splattered across the statistics pages of the Notre Dame record books.

But of the countless fabled names in Notre Dame's football past, the one that still prompts as many questions as any other in the Notre Dame sports information department is that of Montana, quarterback of Notre Dame's 1977 national championship team.

Many visitors to Notre Dame's Heritage Hall are often surprised to discover that Montana never received All-America status and was not selected until the third round of the National Football

League draft. Still, interest in Montana's exploits remains keen partly because of his stardom in the NFL (he was a first-ballot inductee into the Pro Football Hall of Fame and was enshrined in July 2000) and partly because his five years at Notre Dame were so eventful.

So here's a detailed look at Montana's Notre Dame career:

Montana's Career Statistics
(JV in 1974; did not play in 1976 due to injury)

Year	G/GS	Time	PC-PA-Yds	TD/Int	TC-Yds-TD
1975	7/3	92:37	28–66–507	4/8	25-(–5)–2
1977	9/8	198:38	99–189–1604	11/8	32–5–6
1978	11/11	280:30	141–260–2010	10/9	72–104–6
Totals	27/22	571:45	268–515–4121	25/25	129–104–14

Career Averages:
52.0 completion percentage
152.6 passing yards per game

1974
Made his official recruiting visit to Notre Dame the weekend of January 19, 1974, when Notre Dame's basketball team ended the record 88-game winning streak by UCLA...played with Notre Dame junior varsity squad as freshman...completed 1-of-6 passes with one interception for 35 yards, rushed five times for seven yards, and punted 10 times for an average of 36.5 yards...three other quarterbacks—Gary Forystek, Kerry Moriarty, and Mike Falash—attempted more passes than he did during the three-game junior varsity season...did not play with varsity as freshman due to presence of veteran quarterback Tom Clements in Ara Parseghian's final season with Fighting Irish...completed 7-of-12 passes for 131 yards and three touchdowns while staking his claim to the starting job in the 1975 Blue-Gold final spring game.

1975

Shared quarterbacking chores as sophomore with junior Rick Slager under first-year coach Dan Devine…came off the bench for an injured Slager with the Irish down 7–0 to Northwestern, accounting for 108 total yards while throwing for one score and running for the final Irish touchdown in 31–7 win…came off the bench with 6:04 left vs. North Carolina and Notre Dame trailing 14–6 and completed 3-of-4 passes for 129 yards, including game-winning 80-yard touchdown pass to Ted Burgmeier (that ranked as third-longest pass in Irish history) at the 1:03 mark, an earlier 39-yarder to Dan Kelleher, plus a two-point conversion throw in a 21–14 road win…came off the bench with 13:00 left vs. Air Force with the Irish trailing 30–10 and engineered three touchdown drives—running for one touchdown from 3 yards out and passing for another on a 7-yard toss to Ken MacAfee to spark 31–30 comeback win…broke a finger versus Navy and did not play the rest of the year.

Statistics for 1975

Game (* started)	PC-PA-Yds	TD/Int	Result
Boston College	DNP		
Purdue	0–1–0	0/1	W, 17–0
Northwestern	6–11–80	1/0	W, 31–7
*Michigan State	2–5–19	0/1	L, 10–3
North Carolina	3–4–129	1/0	W, 21–14
Air Force	7–18–134	1/3	W, 31–30
*No. 3 USC	3–11–25	0/2	L, 24–17
*Navy	7–16–120	1/1	W, 31–10
Georgia Tech	DNP—broken finger		
Pittsburgh	DNP—broken finger		
Miami	DNP—broken finger		
Totals	28–66–507	4/8	5 W, 2 L

1976

Sat out entire year due to separated shoulder injury suffered in pre-season...was member of championship team in campus Bookstore Basketball tournament the following spring (1977).

1977

An honorable mention Associated Press All-American...started last nine games and never lost, leading Irish to national title with 38–10 win over unbeaten and top-ranked Texas in 1978 Cotton Bowl...began campaign behind Rusty Lisch on depth chart and didn't play in first two games...came off the bench with 11:00 left vs. Purdue and the Irish trailing 24–14, throwing two touchdown

In the famous 1977 green-jersey game, quarterback Joe Montana ran for two touchdowns and threw for two others as the Irish defeated USC 49–19. Montana was named offensive MVP of the game by ABC.

passes in the 31–24 win…started the final 21 games of his Notre Dame career, beginning the following week vs. Michigan State…named by ABC as offensive MVP vs. USC, after running for two touchdowns and throwing for two others in the famous "green-jersey game" (a 49–19 Irish win)…threw for more than 260 yards each of the next two Saturdays vs. Navy and Georgia Tech, the first time an Irish quarterback had done that in seven years…rushed for two fourth-quarter touchdowns in comeback win over Clemson (21–17)…ranked 16th in final NCAA stats for total offense.

Statistics for 1977

Game (* started)	PC-PA-Yds	TD/Int Result
No. 7 Pittsburgh	DNP	
Mississippi	DNP	
Purdue	9–14–154	1/0 W, 31–24
*Michigan State	8–23–105	0/3 W, 16–6
*Army	8–17–109	0/1 W, 24–0
*No. 5 USC	13–24–167	2/1 W, 49–19
*Navy	11–24–260	1/2 W, 43–10
*Georgia Tech 1	5–25–273	3/0 W, 69–14
*No. 15 Clemson	9–21–172	0/0 W, 21–17
*Air Force	11–15–172	1/1 W, 49–0
*Miami	15–26–192	3/0 W, 48–10
Totals	99–189–1604	11/8 9 W
*No. 1 Texas (Cotton Bowl)	10–25–11	1/1 W, 38–10

1978

An honorable mention pick on Associated Press All-America team for second straight year (Penn State's Chuck Fusina was NCAA consensus first-team choice)…became only the third Irish quarterback to throw for more than 2,000 yards in a season…served as a team tri-captain...ranked 14th in final NCAA stats for total offense and 20th in passing...completed his final 10 passes vs. Georgia Tech to tie Irish record set by Angelo Bertelli in 1942...named ABC offensive player of the game vs. ninth-ranked Pittsburgh and USC...helped Irish overcome 17–7 deficit with 13:46 left vs. Pittsburgh by completing seven straight passes—including two for touchdowns—in fourth quarter of 26–17 Irish win...set personal highs with 20 completions, 41 attempts and 358 yards in 27–25 loss at USC in regular-season finale...brought Irish back from 24–6 deficit with 12:59 remaining to give Irish the lead late in game before Trojans won on final field goal...named to United Press International backfield of the week for play vs. USC after completing 17-of-26 second-half passes (after three of 15 in first half)...brought Irish back from 34–12 deficit in 1979 Cotton Bowl vs. Houston, hitting Kris Haines for winning touchdown pass on final play of game in frigid conditions in Dallas.

Statistics for 1978

Game (* started)	PC-PA-Yds	TD/Int Result
*Missouri	13–28–151	0/2 L, 3–0
*No. 5 Michigan	16–29–192	1/2 L, 28–14
*Purdue	7–11–95	0/2 W, 10–6
*Michigan State	6–12–149	0/0 W, 29–25
*No. 9 Pittsburgh	15–25–218	2/0 W, 26–17
*Air Force	13–24–193	2/0 W, 38–15
*Miami	12–20–175	0/1 W, 20–0
*No. 11 Navy	14–26–145	1/1 W, 27–7
*Tennessee	11–25–144	0/0 W, 31–14
*No. 20 Georgia Tech	14–19–190	2/0 W, 38–21
*No. 3 USC	20–41–358	2/1 L, 27–25
Totals	141–260–2010	10/9 8 W, 3 L
*No. 9 Houston (Cotton Bowl)	13–34–163	1/3 W, 35–34

ESPN's award-winning *Sports Century* series placed Montana as the No. 25 North American athlete of the twentieth century in 1998 voting by a 48-member panel of journalists, historians, and administrators. Only two football players placed higher: Jim Brown (No. 4) and multi-sport star Jim Thorpe (No. 7).

Longtime *Sports Illustrated* writer Paul Zimmerman selected Montana as his top professional quarterback for "post-1978 rules," while Johnny Unitas was Zimmerman's pick for the top pro signal-caller prior to 1978. Former Notre Dame tight end Dave Casper was also named to Zimmerman's exclusive NFL All-Century Team.

In polling by visitors to the cnnsi.com Web site, Montana was selected as the "fans' choice favorite NFL player of the century," outdistancing fellow finalist Dick Butkus by better than a 2-to-1 voting margin (68 percent to 32 percent).

The *Sports Illustrated* Web site, SI.com, listed Montana as the seventh greatest Notre Dame athlete of all time in its summer 2008 listings, identifying him as "perhaps Notre Dame's most recognizable football name."

11 The Epic Confrontation

The 1966 Michigan State Game

When the brutal battle in East Lansing was finally over, there was nothing left but inconsolable emptiness and frustration.

The epic battle between top-ranked Notre Dame and No. 2 Michigan State didn't settle much of anything for either team. When the clock ticked its last second-hand sweep, exhausted and battered players, emotionally spent coaches, and frenzied fans could only look at the 10–10 tie in exasperation and disappointment.

"Nobody can be happy with a tie," said Irish quarterback Terry Hanratty, who had to leave the game in the first quarter after Bubba Smith rearranged his shoulder. "It was a helluva ballgame, but we were all so tired. I don't think anyone wanted to go into a fifth quarter."

The Irish, who had rallied from a 10–0 deficit early in the second quarter, had a chance to go for the win. Notre Dame had the ball on its 30-yard line with time for at least four passing plays. The Spartans were expecting the Irish to go for broke. But under coach Ara Parseghian's strict orders, the Irish played it safe.

"We'd fought hard to come back and tie it up," Parseghian explained. "After all that, I didn't want to risk giving it to them cheap. They get reckless and it could cost them the game. I wasn't going to do a jackass thing like that at this point."

His players agreed.

"It was the worst kind of depression coming off the field after working that hard and coming out with a tie," remembered pass-catching sensation Jim Seymour, who didn't catch a pass that afternoon.

"What people don't realize is that we couldn't throw the ball because they had set up a specific defense to stop the pass. Our quarterback was so run down because of his diabetic problem that he couldn't throw the ball more than 10 yards. And they were really set for it. So why throw the ball for an interception and really hang yourself? Ara's been questioned many times about that decision.... But there was nothing else he could do under the circumstances."

Seymour was right. The Irish were probably lucky to survive with a tie. Their best halfback, Nick Eddy, had slipped getting off the train in East Lansing and fell on an already banged-up shoulder. He wouldn't even get in the game. Center George Goeddeke's ankle fell victim to Smith in the first quarter, along with Hanratty.

But Coley O'Brien, who required two insulin shots a day to keep his diabetes in check, and sophomore Bob Gladieux proved able replacements.

After the Spartans had taken a 10–0 lead on Regis Cavender's four-yard run and Dick Kenney's 47-yard field goal, O'Brien directed the Irish 54 yards in four plays. He hit Gladieux with an 11-yard strike and Rocky Bleier for a 9-yard gain. O'Brien then lofted a perfect 34-yard spiral to Gladieux, who caught it on the goal line and stepped into the end zone.

The Irish finally caught up with the Spartans on the first play of the fourth quarter. After Notre Dame stalled on the Michigan State 10-yard line, Joe Azzaro kicked a 28-yard field goal to knot the score. Notre Dame dominated the second half, and the defense didn't let the Spartans any closer than they were when they had kicked the field goal. Linebackers Jim Lynch and Jim Horney nailed the talented Spartan runners for either minus yardage or no yardage on 16 rushing plays.

With five minutes left in the game, the Irish got a big break. Safety Tom Schoen intercepted a wild Jimmy Raye pass and ran it back to the Spartan 18-yard line. Larry Conjar went straight ahead for two yards. But on the second play, halfback Dave Haley went wide to his left. Smith and Phil Hoag nailed him for an eight-yard loss. O'Brien's third-down pass went incomplete, and Notre Dame had to settle for a 42-yard field goal try.

Azzaro's kick went wide to the right.

12 The 1973 Championship Season

Roll Over the Tide Caps Unbeaten Year

Every college football season seems to have its own game of the century, but the 1973 matchup between Notre Dame and Alabama was special. It came in the Sugar Bowl, and it was to be a dream game.

Two undefeated, highly ranked teams with long and storied gridiron traditions were set to battle for the national championship. The prognosticators' predictions rang true as the Fighting Irish emerged 24–23 victors over the Crimson Tide of Alabama in a thriller that saw the lead change hands six times.

Bob Thomas, who had missed two earlier attempts in the game, kicked a 19-yard field goal with 4:26 remaining to give the Irish and coach Ara Parseghian the one-point triumph over top-rated Alabama. The win clinched Notre Dame's sixth wire-service national championship and ninth overall as the Irish finished the season with a perfect 11–0 record.

The balanced Irish attack was keyed by four backs who gained more than 300 yards apiece that season: fullback Wayne Bullock (752), halfback Art Best (700), halfback Eric Penick (586), and quarterback Tom Clements (360). It was one of the fastest back-fields Notre Dame had ever assembled, as Penick had 9.5 speed in the 100-yard dash, while Best checked in at 9.7.

The Irish were ranked in the eighth spot in the polls with wins over Rice and Army, setting the stage for what everyone considered to be Notre Dame's first real test of the year, a home battle with sixth-ranked USC.

The Trojans came to town riding a 23-game unbeaten streak, and Notre Dame was full of memories of the previous season's clash, which saw running back Anthony Davis romp for six touchdowns in a 45–23 Trojan win. Squib kicks were the solution to the problem of Davis returning kicks, and a fired-up defense held him to just 55 yards on 19 carries.

Quite simply, the day belonged to Notre Dame, as Penick ran for 118 yards, 50 more than the entire USC squad. The Irish pulled off a 23–14 win and jumped to fifth in the polls.

Notre Dame cruised through the remainder of the schedule. Navy was an easy victim, 44–7, and No. 20 Pittsburgh played the docile host to the Irish and fell 31–10. The Irish finished off

With its 24–23 victory over Alabama, Notre Dame topped off a perfect 11–0 season and earned the national championship.

Parseghian's first perfect regular season with a 48–15 win over Air Force and a 44–0 whitewashing of Miami at the Orange Bowl.

The stage was set for the contest between No. 1 Alabama and third-ranked Notre Dame that seemed to deserve every phrase of its high-powered buildup. It marked the first-ever meeting between the Irish and Tide—and ESPN college football expert Beano Cook still considers it the best bowl game he's seen. The Irish opened the contest with a superb defensive effort that held the Tide without a yard in the first period as Notre Dame took a 6–0 lead. Alabama's thoroughbred backs made it out of the starting gate in the second period, however. They produced three long drives that resulted in a pair of touchdowns, the first of which put the Tide up 7–6.

Early in the fourth quarter, the game took a wild turn with three turnovers in 90 seconds. Alabama took charge and put in its own version of the razzle-dazzle.

With the ball on the Notre Dame 25, Tide quarterback Richard Todd handed off to halfback Mike Stock (he was from Elkhart, Indiana, maybe 15 miles from the Notre Dame campus), then Todd raced to the sidelines where he took a return pass from Stock and went in for the score. But Alabama missed the conversion try, and the Tide had only a slim two-point lead.

Notre Dame then marched 79 yards in 11 plays. Strong runs by Hunter, Penick, and Clements and a 30-yard pass from Clements to Dave Casper carried the drive to the Alabama 15-yard line. The Irish got to the 3 but couldn't get any closer before the call went to Thomas.

His kick was true, the game belonged to the Irish, and so did the national championship.

13 The Band of the Fighting Irish

All Part of the Tradition

Notre Dame's marching band, appropriately called the Band of the Fighting Irish, is the oldest university band in continual existence and has been on hand for every home game since football started at Notre Dame in 1887.

Notre Dame's band, born in 1845, celebrated its 150th season in 1995. The band was among the first in the nation to include

The Band of the Fighting Irish had already celebrated its 41st anniversary when it took to the field for the football team's first home game against the University of Michigan in 1887. It has not missed a single home game since.

pageantry, precision drill, and now-famous picture formations. It first accepted women from neighboring Saint Mary's College in 1970 before Notre Dame became coeducational in 1972. The band was declared a "landmark of American Music" in 1976 by the National Music Council.

Current band director Ken Dye holds degrees from the University of Houston, Long Beach State, and USC. He has directed bands at Rice and Houston and arranged music performed at the 2000 Olympic Games in Sydney, Australia.

14 Fathers Hesburgh and Joyce

Towering Figures at Notre Dame—and Beyond

Technically, they never worked directly in athletics at Notre Dame.

Still, it's hard to imagine the 35-year tenures of Rev. Theodore M. Hesburgh, C.S.C., as University president and Rev. Edmund P. Joyce, C.S.C., as executive vice president having any greater impact on athletics at the University.

Whether presiding over national championships or coaching hirings or the advent of co-education on campus—and, thus, a women's varsity athletics program—the two of them made their mark not just at Notre Dame but nationally, as well.

Hesburgh became co-chairman of the prestigious Knight Commission that evaluated college athletic philosophy and behavior, and Joyce served as an influential voice in NCAA matters and an officer in the College Football Association that for many years controlled college football television rights and oversaw other aspects of the game.

The duo retired from their positions at Notre Dame on May 31, 1987.

Hesburgh's effect on the University's growth was profound, whether measured in public esteem, academic distinction, physical expansion, or operating budget and endowment. Considered one of the most influential Americans in the areas of education and religion, he has been deeply involved in key social and moral issues, most notably civil rights.

Hesburgh's 35-year term marked the longest of any University president in the country, and he holds a record for receiving 150 honorary degrees. His many distinguished honors include becoming the first recipient (in 2003) of the NCAA's President's Gerald R. Ford Award, honoring an individual who has provided significant leadership as an advocate for intercollegiate athletics on a continuous basis.

Hesburgh served as co-chairman of the Knight Commission on reform of intercollegiate athletics, whose landmark report was issued in March 1991. Nearly a decade after releasing its initial series of reports, the Knight Commission reconvened in 2000 to determine what progress had been made and whether new issues needed to be considered.

During their 35-year tenures at Notre Dame, Rev. Theodore M. Hesburgh, C.S.C. (right) and Rev. Edmund P. Joyce, C.S.C. (left), had a profound impact on athletics on campus and around the country.

Following their joint retirements, Father Hesburgh and the late Father Joyce spent six months touring the country in a mobile home before serving as co-chaplains for a 1988 world cruise on the Queen Elizabeth II. Hesburgh now works out of an office in the Hesburgh Library (named in his honor in 1987) and devotes much of his time to the Institute for International Peace Studies.

Hesburgh was presented with the Congressional Gold Medal in 2000 in Washington, D.C., the highest honor bestowed by Congress. The medal has only been awarded to approximately 300 persons in the history of the republic, with Hesburgh the first recipient from higher education. The medal was created by the U.S. Mint and features Hesburgh's visage on one side while the other side shows images representing his religious community, the Congregation of Holy Cross, and the University of Notre Dame.

Hesburgh added to his distinguished life's work in 2002 when he carried the Olympic torch as it crossed the Notre Dame campus en route to Salt Lake City for the 2002 Winter Olympic Games. He previously received the Medal of Freedom, the nation's highest civilian honor, bestowed by President Lyndon Johnson in 1964. The only other Notre Dame graduate to receive the Congressional Gold Medal was Dr. Thomas Dooley in 1961.

Joyce, whose namesake is Notre Dame's primary athletic facility, the Joyce Center, served as chief financial officer during the Hesburgh presidency. He was born in British Honduras (now Belize) and graduated from Spartanburg (S.C.) High School. He was the first student from South Carolina ever to attend Notre Dame and earned his bachelor's degree in accounting, magna cum laude, in 1937. He worked with the L.C. Dodge accounting firm in Spartanburg and became a certified public accountant in '39.

He entered Holy Cross College in Washington, D.C.—then the C.S.C.'s theological house of studies—in 1945 and was ordained to the priesthood in 1949 at Notre Dame's Sacred Heart Church. After ordination, Joyce was named Notre Dame's assistant vice president for business affairs and then acting vice president in 1949. His tenure was interrupted by a year of advanced study at Oxford University in England. He returned in '51 as vice president for business affairs and in '52 was elevated to executive vice president, also serving as chairman of the Faculty Board on Athletics and the University building committee.

Joyce was an influential voice in the NCAA, particularly dealing with educational integrity in college athletics. He was instrumental in forming the College Football Association and served as secretary-treasurer. The National Football Foundation honored him with its Distinguished American Award.

President Eisenhower appointed Joyce to the Board of Visitors of the U.S. Naval Academy, and the U.S. Air Force awarded him an Exceptional Service Medal. He was inducted into the Indiana Academy in 1990, and three endowed chairs were established in his name at Notre Dame. After retirement, Father Joyce served as honorary chair of the Badin Guild, a planned giving organization for benefactors who provide estate gifts to the University. He was also a life trustee of the University.

Frank Leahy

They Called Him "The Master"
Frank Leahy's very first Notre Dame team in 1941 finished unbeaten.

His last Notre Dame team in 1953 also finished unbeaten.

Frank Leahy learned about winning from the best—he played for Knute Rockne and graduated from Notre Dame in 1931. As head football coach, Leahy's all-time winning percentage (.864) is second only to Rockne.

In between, Leahy's Irish produced four consensus national championship seasons. So it should be no surprise that Leahy remains the second-winningest coach in the history of college football.

He produced six Notre Dame teams that finished without a loss. Nine of his 11 teams ended up sixth or higher in the final Associated Press polls. His 11 years in South Bend produced 87 victories against only 11 defeats—and his all-time winning percentage of .864 (including two seasons as coach at Boston College in 1939–40, producing a 20–2 combined mark and Cotton and Sugar Bowl appearances) remains second in college football history behind only Knute Rockne.

Along the way, Leahy coached four Heisman Trophy winners in Angelo Bertelli, John Lujack, Leon Hart, and John Lattner. And he coached a pair of Outland Trophy winners in George Connor and Bill Fischer. On 20 occasions Leahy's players were selected as consensus All-Americans—and 13 Notre Dame players that he coached are now in the College Football Hall of Fame.

After World War II, Leahy's Irish teams put together one of the more remarkable runs in the history of college football. In 1946, Notre Dame finished 8–0–1, followed by a perfect 9–0 season in '47. In 1948, the Irish finished 9–0–1 and then in '49 a perfect 10–0. So in those four combined seasons, the Irish went 36–0–2. The seniors on the '49 squad like Hart, Jim Martin, and Emil Sitko spent four years at Notre Dame and never lost a football game.

Known as a stern taskmaster, Leahy's practices were often more demanding than the games. But his players loved him—they created the Leahy's Lads group that erected the Leahy sculpture (dedicated September 19, 1997) on the east side of Notre Dame Stadium, and they continue to raise money for scholarships at the University.

A tackle on Rockne's last three Notre Dame teams and a 1931 graduate, Leahy was selected to the National Football Foundation Hall of Fame in 1970. Before becoming a head coach he had been an assistant at Georgetown, Michigan State, and Fordham. He missed two seasons at Notre Dame (1944 and '45) while serving as a lieutenant in the navy during World War II.

A recent edition of the *NCAA Official Football Records Book* listed 12 major college dynasties from the twentieth century "because of historical significance, and all represent an outstanding record as well as at least one national championship." One of those was Notre Dame's 1946–53 period when Leahy was head coach.

16 John Lujack

The All-Purpose Irish Legend

John Lujack took over at quarterback for Notre Dame as a sopho-more in 1943 when Angelo Bertelli joined the U.S. Marines—and he ended up helping the Irish to three national titles while establishing a reputation as one of the great T-formation signal-callers in college football history.

In his initial start, versus Army in 1943, Lujack threw for two scores, ran for another, and intercepted a pass in a 26–0 victory. He spent nearly three years in the navy but returned in time to earn consensus All-America honors as a junior and senior on Notre Dame teams in 1946 and '47 that did not lose a game.

No slouch as a runner (he also played halfback as a sophomore), Lujack also punted—and probably made his most-remembered and maybe greatest individual play on defense. He preserved a scoreless tie in 1946 between the second-ranked Irish and top-ranked Army from his defensive back position by making a touchdown-saving tackle of Cadet star fullback Doc Blanchard.

As a junior, the 6'0", 180-pounder from Connellsville, Pennsylvania, finished third in the Heisman voting behind Army's Glenn Davis. As a senior, he earned the Associated Press Male Athlete of the Year award. He won the 1947 Heisman Trophy with 742 votes—compared to 555 for Michigan's Bob Chappuis and 196 for SMU's Doak Walker.

His career numbers included 144 completions of 280 attempts for 2,080 yards and 19 touchdowns, plus 81 rushing carries for 438 yards and two touchdowns. As a senior in his Heisman campaign, he was 61-of-109 passing for 777 yards and nine touchdowns, plus 12 running attempts for 139 yards and one score.

Lujack played four years with the Chicago Bears, leading the team in scoring each year, tying a record with eight interceptions as a rookie, throwing for a record 468 yards in one game in 1949, and playing in the NFL Pro Bowl his last two seasons.

An Irish backfield coach for two years following his retirement in 1952, Lujack then ran an automobile dealership in Davenport, Iowa, until he retired in 1988.

ESPN's Beano Cook and longtime *Sports Illustrated* college football expert Dan Jenkins tabbed him as their selection for best all-time quarterback. Lujack rated as the top defensive back by longtime *Dallas Times-Herald* and *Dallas Morning News* columnist Blackie Sherrod. In its 2008 book, *The College Football Book*, *Sports Illustrated* selected Lujack as a first-team back on its 1940s all-decade squad.

He was elected to the National Football Foundation Hall of Fame in 1960. Lujack has also made several donations to the University to establish an academic scholarship endowment.

17 Walk from Basilica to Stadium

Your Chance to Follow Irish Footsteps

The pregame routine on gamedays for Notre Dame football has always featured a Mass. On the road, it's a simple religious ceremony reserved for players and coaches in a hotel ballroom just before the Irish board buses bound for the stadium. At home, Mass has been held at a variety of locations—from Moreau Seminary, where for years the team stayed on Friday nights prior to home games, to several residence hall chapels.

Two hours prior to kickoff, the players walk from Mass at the Basilica to the Stadium.

Eventually the pregame masses were moved to the Basilica of the Sacred Heart in the middle of campus, after which the players walk as a group from the Basilica to Notre Dame Stadium about two hours prior to kickoff.

The prescribed path of the Notre Dame players now is so well known that thousands of fans ring the sidewalks and walkways as the Irish players, dressed in coats and ties, head to do battle. The fans aren't shy about reaching out to the players, both physically and by exhorting them to victory.

Wander by the quadrangle between the Basilica and the Stadium some Saturday. You'll enjoy a different look at the Irish undergraduates you're used to seeing in helmets and shoulder pads.

18 The Four Horsemen

A Nickname with Staying Power

A nickname coined by a poetic sportswriter and the quick-thinking actions of a clever student publicity aide transformed the Notre Dame backfield of Stuhldreher, Crowley, Miller, and Layden into the most fabled quartet in college football history.

Quarterback Harry Stuhldreher, left halfback Jim Crowley, right halfback Don Miller, and fullback Elmer Layden had run rampant through Irish opponents' defenses since coach Knute Rockne devised the lineup in 1922 during their sophomore season. But the foursome needed some help from Grantland Rice, a sportswriter for the *New York Herald-Tribune*, to achieve football immortality.

After Notre Dame's 13–7 victory over Army on October 18, 1924, Rice penned the most famous passage in the history of sports journalism.

"Outlined against a blue, gray October sky the Four Horsemen rode again.

"In dramatic lore they are known as famine, pestilence, destruction, and death. These are only aliases. Their real names are: Stuhldreher, Miller, Crowley, and Layden. They formed the crest of the South Bend cyclone before which another fighting Army team was swept over the precipice at the Polo Grounds this afternoon as 55,000 spectators peered down upon the bewildering panorama spread out upon the green plain below."

George Strickler, then Rockne's student publicity aide and later sports editor of the *Chicago Tribune*, made sure the name stuck. In fact, he had watched the movie, *The Four Horsemen of the Apocalypse* starring Rudolph Valentino the night before the football game—and Rice overheard Strickler mention that tidbit in the press box.

After the team arrived back in South Bend, Rice posed the four players, dressed in their uniforms, on the backs of four horses from a livery stable in town. The wire services picked up the now-famous photo, and the legendary status of the Four Horsemen was insured.

The 1999 season marked the 75th anniversary of the Four Horsemen's senior year, and descendants of each member of that group were honored at the Notre Dame vs. Navy game on October 30, 1999.

"At the time, I didn't realize the impact it would have," Crowley said later. "But the thing just kind of mushroomed. After the splurge in the press, the sports fans of the nation got interested in us along with other sportswriters. Our record helped, too. If we'd lost a couple, I don't think we would have been remembered."

After that win over Army, Notre Dame's third straight victory of the young season, the Irish were rarely threatened the rest of the year. A 27–10 win over Stanford in the 1925 Rose Bowl gave Rockne and Notre Dame the national championship and a perfect 10–0 record.

As it usually is with legends, the Four Horsemen earned their spot in gridiron history.

Although none of the four stood taller than 6' and none of the four weighed more than 162 pounds, the Four Horsemen might comprise the greatest backfield ever. As a unit, Stuhldreher, Crowley, Miller, and Layden played 30 games and only lost to one team, Nebraska, twice.

Stuhldreher, a 5'7", 151-pounder from Massillon, Ohio, was a self-assured leader who not only could throw accurately but also returned punts and proved a solid blocker. He emerged as the starting quarterback four games into his sophomore season in 1922. He

No, they weren't famine, pestilence, destruction, and death—they were Stuhldreher, Miller, Crowley, and Layden. And their heroic on-field exploits during Notre Dame's 13–7 victory over Army on October 18, 1924, immortalized the quartet as the Four Horsemen.

was often labeled cocky, feisty, and ambitious, but his field-general skill was unmatched.

Crowley, who came to Notre Dame in 1921 from Green Bay, Wisconsin, stood 5'11" and weighed 162 pounds. Known as "Sleepy Jim" for his drowsy-eyed appearance, Crowley outmaneuvered many a defender with his clever, shifty ballcarrying.

Miller, a native of Defiance, Ohio, followed his three brothers to Notre Dame. At 5'11", 160 pounds, he proved to be the team's breakaway threat. According to Rockne, Miller was the greatest open-field runner he ever coached.

Layden, the fastest of the quartet, became the Irish defensive star with his timely interceptions, and he also handled punting chores. The 6'0", 162-pounder from Davenport, Iowa, boasted 10-second speed in the 100-yard dash.

After graduation, the lives of the Four Horsemen took similar paths. All began coaching careers with three of the four occupying top positions.

Layden coached at his alma mater for seven years and compiled a 47–13–3 record. He also served as athletics director at Notre Dame. After a business career in Chicago, Layden died in 1973 at age 70.

Crowley coached Vince Lombardi at Fordham before entering business in Cleveland. He died in 1986 at age 83.

Stuhldreher, who died in 1965 at age 63, became athletics director and football coach at Wisconsin.

Miller left coaching after four years at Georgia Tech and began practicing law in Cleveland. He was appointed U.S. District Attorney for Northern Ohio by President Franklin D. Roosevelt. Miller died in 1979 at age 77.

All four players were elected to the National Football Foundation Hall of Fame—Layden in 1951, Stuhldreher in 1958, Crowley in 1966, and Miller in 1970.

The Four Horsemen were featured in 1998 on one of 15 commemorative postage stamps that saluted "The Roaring Twenties" as part of the Celebrate the Century program by the United States Postal Service. The stamp was unveiled in ceremonies at the College Football Hall of Fame in South Bend on May 19, 1998, and the stamp went on sale nationally as part of the series on May 30, 1998. Celebrate the Century was a commemorative stamp and education program honoring some of the most memorable and significant people, places, events, and trends of each decade of the twentieth century.

The *Sports Illustrated* Web site, SI.com, rated the Four Horsemen the fourth greatest Notre Dame athletes of all-time (behind George Gipp, Paul Hornung, and Brady Quinn) in its summer 2008 listings.

19 Sugar is Sweet

The 1973 Sugar Bowl vs. Alabama

It was to be a dream game.

Two undefeated, highly ranked teams with long and storied gridiron traditions were set to battle for the national championship. It was billed as a classic confrontation—the (latest) game of the century.

The prognosticators' predictions rang true as the 1973 Sugar Bowl saw third-ranked Notre Dame emerge a 24–23 winner over top-rated Alabama in a thriller that saw the lead change hands six times.

Bob Thomas, who had missed two attempts earlier in the game, kicked a 19-yard field goal with 4:26 remaining to give the Fighting Irish and coach Ara Parseghian the one-point upset over Alabama. The win also clinched the national championship for Notre Dame, which finished the season at 11–0.

The Sugar Bowl record crowd of 85,161 was treated to a pulsating battle that went to the wire. With three minutes to play, Alabama's punting specialist, Greg Gantt, booted a 69-yard punt that backed up the Irish to their own 1-yard line. However, Gantt was fouled on the play and Alabama was entitled to keep the ball with fourth-and-5.

But Alabama's Paul "Bear" Bryant elected to decline the penalty, hoping his defense could force an Irish turnover deep in their own territory. Moments later, Notre Dame quarterback Tom Clements rifled a pass to tight end Robin Weber at the 38 and secured the national championship. A famous Rich Clarkson photo (see p. 41), taken from behind Clements in the end zone as the throw was made, memorializes that signature play.

The Irish opened the contest with a superb defensive effort that held the Tide without a yard gained in the first period. Led by Clements, who shot passes of 19, 26, and 14 yards to split end Pete Demmerle, the Irish offense drew first blood in the opening period. Fullback Wayne Bullock capped a 64-yard scoring drive with a six-yard gallop into the end zone.

Alabama's thoroughbred backs made it out of the starting gate in the second period. They produced three long drives that resulted in a pair of scores—the first coming with 7:30 remaining. Randy Billingsley scored on a six-yard run, and Bill Davis added the extra point that put Alabama up by one at 7–6.

On the ensuing kickoff, Notre Dame's Al Hunter stunned the crowd with his dazzling 93-yard return, the longest in Sugar Bowl history. The Irish went for two and converted as Clements hit Demmerle in the end zone for a 14–7 Notre Dame lead.

Alabama moved deep into Notre Dame territory late in the second quarter but had to settle for a 39-yard field goal by Davis.

At the start of the second half, Alabama marched 93 yards and took the lead on Wilbur Jackson's five-yard scoring plunge. Again Notre Dame charged back, but a 54-yard field goal try by Thomas fell by the wayside.

Notre Dame excited the crowd again when linebacker Drew Mahalic recovered a Tide fumble in mid-air and took the ball to the Alabama 12-yard line. On the first play from scrimmage, Eric Penick dashed 12 yards for the score. Thomas' kick gave the Irish a 21–17 lead.

Early in the fourth period, the game took a zany turn with three turnovers in 90 seconds. Alabama took charge and put in its own version of the razzle-dazzle. With the ball on the Notre Dame 25, second-string quarterback Richard Todd handed off to halfback Mike Stock, then raced to the sidelines where he took a return pass from Stock and went in for the score. But Davis missed the conversion try and Bryant's Tide, which hadn't won a bowl game in its last four appearances, hung on to a slim two-point advantage.

Notre Dame then marched 79 yards in 11 plays. Strong runs by Hunter, Penick, and Clements, and a 30-yard pass from Clements to Dave Casper carried the drive to the Alabama 15-yard line. The Irish got to the 3-yard line but couldn't get any closer when the call went to Thomas. This time he didn't miss, and the Irish had a 24–23 win.

The Sporting News judged four games involving Notre Dame among the top-10 college football games of the 1900s (November 6, 1999, edition). The only other schools with multiple entries were Miami (three), Nebraska (two), and Oklahoma (two). Here's how the magazine described its selections of games involving Notre Dame:

- No. 4—1973 Sugar Bowl (ND 24, Alabama 23): "First meeting ever between giants of college football; Irish march 79 yards in 11 plays to set up game-winning FG; Tom Clements ices it with 35-yard, third-down pass to Robin Weber from 2-yard line."
- No. 5—1935 (ND 18, Ohio State 13): "Top-ranked Buckeyes heavily favored; OSU leads 13–0 in 4th quarter, Irish draw to 13–12 late, but fail to recover onside kick; OSU fumbles and backup QB Bill Shakespeare throws touchdown pass."
- No. 6—1988 (ND 31, Miami 30): "Irish snap Miami's 36-game, regular-season winning streak when Pat Terrell knocks down Steve Walsh's two-point conversion with 0:45 left…"

- No. 8—1979 Cotton Bowl (ND 35, Houston 34): "Joe Montana, out most of 3rd quarter with below-normal body temperature, rallies Irish from 34–12 deficit in final 7:37; Montana ties it with touchdown pass on last play; PAT gives ND win."

20 The 1988 Miami Game

Holtz Promised—And Then Delivered

The edge of the seats in Notre Dame Stadium may be worn thin, but the Stadium's magic remains alive and well. The same could be said for Notre Dame's football program.

That was the end result when Pat Terrell batted away Steve Walsh's two-point conversion pass with 45 seconds to play, as the fourth-rated Irish locked up a stunning 31–30 upset of No. 1-ranked Miami in 1988.

Erased was Miami's mystique and all the embarrassment it had handed the Irish in recent years.

The game had such an impact on Irish fans that they rated it the top moment in Irish history in the twentieth century as part of Notre Dame's "Century of Greatness" program. And it came after head coach Lou Holtz had predicted victory the night before at a wild, outdoor pep rally (later claiming "you should never be held responsible for what you say at a pep rally").

Walsh had his most prolific day and found himself saddled with his first loss in 17 college starts. The Miami regular-season winning streak ended at 36 games, and its road win streak ended at 20. Notre Dame had lost the previous four emotional encounters by a

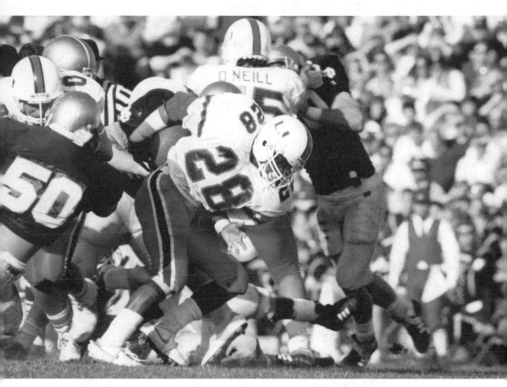

In one of the most stunning finishes in team history, Lou Holtz's Notre Dame squad upset No. 1 Miami, 31–30, in their 1988 contest.

133–20 margin—but the Irish made those losses seem like ancient history with the one-point triumph.

Both clubs made mistakes and caused mistakes. Yet Notre Dame made the big play that counted.

Its defense was on the spot in the final two minutes.

The Irish led 31–24 when Tony Rice was hit hard to force a fumble on third-and-17 from the 21. The Hurricanes' Greg Mark recovered and the Irish were in trouble.

Miami gained four yards in three plays, then faced a fourth-and-6 from the 11. Walsh, who completed 31-of-50 for 424 yards, four touchdowns, and three interceptions, lofted a pass to the right front corner of the end zone, and Andre Brown made a lunging reception for the touchdown. Miami coach Jimmy Johnson said there was never any doubt about the choice of going for the two-point conversion.

Walsh dropped back and had time. But when pressure came from Irish tackle George Williams, he lofted the pass toward tailback Leonard Conley in the end zone. Terrell, in man-to-man coverage, had him blanketed and stepped in front to knock it away. Miami went with an onside-kick attempt—the Hurricanes had won at Michigan, 31–30, after recovering an onside kick—but Anthony Johnson smothered it at the Miami 44. All Notre Dame had to do was ride out 42 seconds to sign another chapter to its glorious history.

For the most part, the Irish couldn't stop Miami unless it took the ball away. It did seven times—three on interceptions and four on fumble recoveries. The Irish gave it back three times.

The most controversial Miami miscue came with seven minutes to go. On fourth-and–7 at the Irish 11, Walsh hit Cleveland Gary with a short pass. Strong safety George Streeter hit Gary near the end zone, and the ball popped loose at the 1. Michael Stonebreaker recovered.

Notre Dame, shuffling in eight offensive linemen because of injuries, drew first blood with a 75-yard, 12-play drive capped by Rice's seven-yard run.

Walsh answered early in the second quarter when he drove the Hurricanes 68 yards in eight plays. Brown caught the eight-yard touchdown pass for a 7–7 tie.

Notre Dame got a couple in the second quarter. Rice hooked up with Raghib Ismail on a 57-yard pass on third-and-13 from the Irish 17, then finished off the 80-yard drive with a nine-yard scoring toss to Braxston Banks.

Less than two minutes later, Terrell stepped in front of a Walsh pass that was tipped by defensive end Frank Stams and returned it

60 yards for the score. Reggie Ho's third PAT gave the Irish a 21–7 lead.

Walsh only needed five minutes to erase it, ending one drive with a 23-yard touchdown pass to Conley on fourth-and-5, and the other on a 15-yard pass to Gary.

The Irish could have felt good about the halftime tie—had it not been for the ease with which Miami punched in its second and third touchdowns.

They started over at the half, and it got crazier. Rice was intercepted by Bubba McDowell at the Miami 42. But on first down, Conley was hammered by Jeff Alm and Stams recovered the fumble.

The Irish got into field-goal range, but Bill Hackett's 43-yard attempt was blocked.

The Irish defense held. On fourth-and-3 at the 47, Miami tried a fake punt and failed. Reserve quarterback Steve Belles made the stop on upback Matt Britton. From the 46, the Irish took two plays to get in. Rice and Ricky Watters hooked up on a 44-yard pass play, and Pat Eilers went the final two yards.

Miami drove again to the Irish 25 when Alm at 6–6 picked off a Walsh pass two yards off the line. The Irish took the momentum and marched 65 yards in nine plays before stalling at the 11. Ho hit the 27-yarder to give the Irish their 31–21 lead.

Miami made good on its first possession of the final quarter when Carlos Huerta hit a 23-yard field goal to close the gap to 31–24.

In 2003, CollegeFootballNews.com produced its list of the 100 Best College Football Finishes since 1970, and the 1988 classic between the Irish and Miami at Notre Dame Stadium was ranked fifth in that survey.

21 The 1993 Florida State Game

The Stadium's Most-Hyped Ever

This was one matchup where the game lived up to the pregame hype, maybe even beat it. Notre Dame and Florida State entered this latest Game of the Century with undefeated records, identical 16-game winning streaks, and the top two rankings in the Associated Press poll (the Seminoles held the top spot).

The buildup for this game was at an all-time high, thanks in part to the two teams entering the game undefeated—and thanks in part to the ever-expanding electronic and print media. As each week during the college football season went by, and as the Fighting Irish and Seminoles both remained unblemished, it became clear that November 13 was not going to be just another football game at Notre Dame Stadium.

National media began rolling in for this event on Monday, and by the time kickoff came on Saturday, more than 700 media credentials were issued. Personalities from television talk show host Regis Philbin to movie producer Spike Lee converged on Notre Dame Stadium, as did athletes like baseball's Roger Clemens and golf's Paul Azinger. On Friday night, the Joyce Athletic and Convocation Center was jam-packed for a pep rally two hours before it was scheduled to start.

And through all the hype, all the glitter, all the celebrities, the most exciting part of the whole week was undoubtedly clear—the actual 60 minutes of football played on the Notre Dame Stadium turf.

"I thought with all the hype, the game might not live up to it," said Notre Dame coach Lou Holtz. "I don't know how it looked from the press box, and I don't know how it looked from the stands.

But I want to tell you I wouldn't want it any more exciting from the sidelines. I can promise you that."

After controlling and leading most of the game, it all came down—as if the football gods wanted to put a spike in the heart of the hype once and for all—to the final play before the Irish won 31–24.

With three seconds left to play, Florida State quarterback and eventual Heisman Trophy winner Charlie Ward had one last chance.

The previous series, on a fourth-and-goal from the 20, Ward had found a miracle by hitting Kez McCorvey for a touchdown pass that had bounced off the hands of Notre Dame safety Brian Magee to cut the lead to seven with 1:39 left to play.

After a three-and-out series for the Irish, Florida State got the ball back with 51 seconds remaining, no timeouts, and the ball at its own 37. Three plays and 41 seconds later, the Seminoles were at the Irish 14, and Ward's first try for the touchdown was batted down by defensive end Thomas Knight.

That left three seconds and one play.

"I was scared a little bit there," said Irish quarterback Kevin McDougal. "You can have no control when you're on the sidelines, and with Charlie Ward on the field, anything can happen. I had watched the drive where they got the touchdown before so I said I'll switch up and not watch it. I just watched the clock and on the last play I waited for the crowd reaction."

He liked what he heard because here's what everyone else in Notre Dame Stadium saw. Ward went back, got some pressure from the Irish defensive line, scrambled, and fired for the end zone toward Kevin Knox. Notre Dame cornerback Shawn Wooden, inserted as a sixth defensive back, batted the pass down and bedlam followed.

"We had to throw the ball in the end zone," Ward said. "I missed my guy who was wide open [Matt Frier at the 5], but that's part of making the decision and the ball was batted down. I can't go back and rethink what I did."

Said Wooden, "Coach Holtz just told us to stay fundamentally sound, read your keys. Charlie came to my side. I looked at No. 1, he did a square-in, so I just stayed underneath. When Ward was scrambling, I just tried to stay under No. 1. I was staying there, no matter what.

"The pass was right to me. I was surprised. I just wanted to knock it down and make sure."

Florida State scored on its first possession and then was chasing from behind for the rest of the afternoon. The Irish came right back with an 80-yard drive capped by a 32-yard romp on a reverse by Adrian Jarrell behind the escort of linemen Aaron Taylor, Ryan Leahy, and Todd Norman downfield.

A 26-yard touchdown run by Lee Becton keyed the second Irish drive, and three minutes later the Irish cashed in on John Covington's interception. Coupled with a personal foul on Florida State, Notre Dame took over on the Seminoles 23, and a third-down pass to Michael Miller from McDougal set up a six-yard touchdown run by Jeff Burris. Entering the game, the Seminoles had given up just two rushing touchdowns the entire season.

"I've got no excuses about the game. Notre Dame won the game. I thought they deserved to win the game," said Florida State head coach Bobby Bowden. "They did the things to us I was afraid they were going to do to us. And there's no doubt about the great spirit they have here. I think it helps them. I do not think it hurt us. Their kids just played possessed."

By halftime it was 21–7 Irish, marking the first time in 23 games that the Seminoles had been behind at the half. Ward had been picked off for just the second time in the season, breaking a streak of 159 passes without an interception. It didn't get any better for the Seminoles in the third quarter, as the Irish received a 47-yard field goal from Kevin Pendergast.

But Ward, who was 31-of-50 for 297 yards and three touchdowns, led Florida State back with an 80-yard scoring drive, concluded with a six-yard pass to Warrick Dunn. Scott Bentley made a 24-yard field goal with 10:40 left for a 24–17 score.

McDougal then went to work through the air. Becton made a one-handed catch on a screen that was good for 15 yards and, on third down, McDougal double-clutched and stepped under a heavy blitz to find Lake Dawson for a first down, setting up Burris' second touchdown of the day.

"Just when it looked like we were going to give them a knockout, they came right back and then it looked like we were on the ropes and we put on a 80-yard drive against the wind," Holtz said.

Becton led all rushers in the game with 122 yards, while McDougal was 9-of-18 in the air for the Irish for 108 yards.

Leon Hart

Irish Lineman Never Lost a Game

Leon Hart and Larry Kelley of Yale (the 1936 recipient) rank as the only linemen ever to win the Heisman Trophy. Joining Irish teammate and tackle Jim Martin as the last of the two-way players with the advent of two-platoon football, Hart gained a reputation as an outstanding blocker and superb rusher on defense in addition to his estimable pass-catching skills.

A four-time letter-winner, Hart never played on the losing side during his years in a Notre Dame uniform—the Irish went 36–0–2 and claimed three national championships. Hart became a three-time, first-team All-American and a consensus choice as a junior and senior.

Lineman Leon Hart was a four-time letterman for Notre Dame and one of only two linemen ever to win the Heisman Trophy.

In 1949, the 6'4", 245-pounder from Turtle Creek, Pennsylvania, was voted the Associated Press Male Athlete of the Year, outpointing such famous names as Jackie Robinson and Sam Snead. He also received the Maxwell Award as top collegiate player in 1949. A mechanical engineering major, Hart called defensive signals and often played fullback as a senior to confuse defenses.

Hart's Heisman-winning season in 1949 ended with him receiving 995 votes, compared to 272 for North Carolina's Charlie Justice and 229 for SMU's Doak Walker (who had also finished third the previous season behind winner John Lujack). Hart's victory marked Notre Dame's third Heisman win—and its third of the decade following Angelo Bertelli in '43 and Lujack in '48.

In its 2008 title *The College Football Book, Sports Illustrated* selected Hart as a first-team end on its all-time team (the only Irish player on the squad) and also named him to its 1940s all-decade squad first unit at end.

Hart went on to play eight seasons with the Detroit Lions, helping the team to three NFL titles and earning all-pro honors on both offense and defense in 1951.

Moving to Birmingham, Michigan, Hart headed up a variety of business enterprises, including the manufacture of tire-balancing equipment.

He was elected to the National Football Foundation and Hall of Fame in 1973. Hart's son Kevin played for the Irish from 1977–79 and his grandson, Brendan, also played for the Irish.

Hart died on September 24, 2002.

Fifth to First

The 1978 Cotton Bowl vs. No. 1 Texas

Then there were none.

Not one unbeaten football team in major college football remained.

Dan Devine's Fighting Irish of Notre Dame took care of the last one, using an unrelenting defense to force six Texas turnovers and an opportunistic offense that capitalized on five of them to rout the previously unbeaten Longhorns 38–10 in the Cotton Bowl and claim the 1977 national championship.

The victory elevated Notre Dame into the top spot in both the Associated Press and United Press International final polls. Meanwhile, Texas—which had held the No. 1 ranking in both polls coming into the game—slipped to No. 4 in AP and No. 5 in UPI.

The Irish were devastating, particularly in the trenches, where the Irish defensive line threw a lasso around Texas Heisman Trophy winner Earl Campbell. Though Campbell did gain 116 yards on 29 carries, they were all tough yards. His longest run from scrimmage late in the second quarter was only 18 yards.

The Irish also forced the Longhorns into six turnovers, three fumbles, and three interceptions, and they took advantage of what Texas gave them with an awesome offensive line performance.

Backs Jerome Heavens and Vagas Ferguson gained 101 and 100 yards, respectively, by going where the Longhorns weren't. Ferguson, who also scored three touchdowns, won the outstanding offensive player honor.

Defensively, the top honor went to Irish middle linebacker Bob Golic, who made 17 tackles and blocked a field-goal attempt by Russell Erxleben.

After the teams had traded field goals in the first quarter— Notre Dame's Dave Reeve hit a 47-yarder (after a Texas fumble), before Erxleben connected on a 42-yarder into a 12-mile-per-hour wind—Golic and teammates Mike Calhoun and Doug Becker forced a Ham Jones fumble on a screen pass from Randy McEachern, and Jim Browner recovered at the Longhorn 27.

Senior captain Terry Eurick scored on the fifth play after that turnover to give the Irish a 10–3 lead on the first play of the second quarter.

Defensive tackle Ken Dike then got into the act on Texas' next possession, stripping a scrambling McEachern of the ball, which Willie Fry recovered at the Longhorn 35.

Five plays later, Eurick scampered in from the 10 for a 17–3 lead. An interception by linebacker Becker set up Notre Dame's third touchdown of the period, a 17-yard pass from Joe Montana to Ferguson.

But the Longhorns threw a scare into the Irish late in the quarter when McEachern directed a 68-yard, six-play drive in just 22 seconds to score. The touchdown came on a 13-yard aerial from McEachern to Mike Lockett after Irish safety Jim Browner had been called for interference on the last play of the first half.

The Irish regained the lost momentum when linebacker Steve Heimkreiter intercepted a McEachern pass midway through the third quarter. Ferguson went the final three yards on the 29-yard drive off left tackle to score, making it 31–10.

The loss ended a storybook season for first-year coach Fred Akers whose Longhorns had won 11 straight games. Notre Dame survived an early loss to Mississippi to finish 11–1 with 10 straight victories—with Eurick appearing on the cover of *Sports Illustrated* the next week to fete the Irish win.

The 1930 Championship Season

Rockne's Last Hurrah

Brand new stadium, same old result—another national championship for the Notre Dame football team.

The 1930 football season marked the opening of Notre Dame Stadium, just another in the long line of Knute Rockne masterpieces, only this was a football stadium instead of a team. With typical meticulosity, he had supervised every minute detail of the construction of the stadium.

In addition, Rockne had for the first time a full-time equipment manager, a trainer, a doctor who traveled with the team, a

The dominant 1930 Notre Dame team earned a second consecutive national championship.

business manager, several secretaries, and a staff to handle the complex sale and distribution of tickets. On top of all that, Rockne was healthy again. The doctors at the Mayo Clinic had given him a thorough going-over from head to foot during the off-season and had given him a clean bill of health. All the Rock had to do was coach, and what a job he did.

On October 4, 1930, the Fighting Irish opened their season in the imposing new stadium—an impressive amphitheatre of sandy-colored brick trimmed with limestone. Rockne had the original sod from Cartier Field transplanted just for good measure.

The Irish christened the good earth with a 20–14 win over Southern Methodist. The stadium was officially dedicated the following week as Notre Dame trounced Navy, 26–2. In the third week of the season, Notre Dame played its third straight home game, defeating Carnegie Tech, 21–6, to cap off a successful first homestand.

Preseason national prognosticators considered the 1930 Notre Dame team to be Rockne's strongest yet. Rockne had said as much himself prior to the start of the season, and he had good reason for such high expectations. Frank Carideo, Marchy Schwartz, Marty Brill, and Joe Savoldi made up a latter-day version of the Four Horsemen in the backfield, and all of them earned All-America status on one team or another for that season.

The Fighting Irish not only were stocked with an explosive collection of running backs, but the team also sported a tremendous crew of linemen. Center Tommy Yarr, guards Nordy Hoffmann and Bert Metzger, tackles Joe Kurth and Al Culver, and end Tom Conley all made All-America teams either that season or the following one.

The Irish left home three times in the fourth-through-eighth weeks of the season but continued to roll. Notre Dame traveled to Pitt and beat the Panthers 35–19. A 27–0 romp over Indiana followed before the Irish visited a 60–20 walloping on Pennsylvania. Marty Brill, who had transferred to Notre Dame from Penn, played the greatest game of his career that day, breaking loose for three touchdowns on runs of 45, 52, and 65 yards.

The Notre Dame winning streak stood at 15 games over two seasons, and it quickly grew to 17 as the Irish sprinted past Drake and Northwestern. All that remained between Notre Dame and another national title were games against Army and USC.

On a November 29 afternoon that saw rain and sleet turn Soldier Field into a swamp, the Cadets and the Irish squared off, and it appeared that neither team was going to budge. Near the end of the game, however, Schwartz broke loose for a 54-yard scoring run. The all-important extra point gave the Irish a 7–0 lead. Army scored quickly thereafter though on a blocked punt, and it appeared that things would be knotted up. But Notre Dame blocked the extra point, and that's the way it ended.

To finish off the season, Rockne used all his psychological expertise in a ploy that helped the Irish get ready for USC. Injuries during the season left the team with only one healthy fullback, Dan Hanley. So Rock decided to turn Bucky O'Connor, a second-team halfback, into a first-string fullback. However, in practice, Rock had O'Connor and Hanley trade jerseys, and not a single soul suspected anything unusual.

When the game got underway, Notre Dame had one of the speediest fullbacks the Trojan defense had ever seen. O'Connor scored two touchdowns, including one on an 80-yard dash, and the Irish dominated the favored home team to the tune of 27–0.

It was a fitting script to what turned out to be Rockne's final game as the Notre Dame head football coach.

The team won its second consecutive national championship, and that winter Rockne died in a plane crash in Kansas.

25 The 1949 Championship Season

End of an Amazing Run

November 15, 1945, ranks as one of the most important dates in Notre Dame football history. Check the record books, though, and you won't find one of the greatest games in Irish history played on that day.

November 15, 1945, was a Thursday, not a Saturday, and that was the day Lieutenant Frank Leahy was discharged from the navy. He returned to Notre Dame campus, signed a 10-year contract, and began what was to be one of the most successful four-year runs in college football history.

The 1946 and 1947 seasons brought national championships to Notre Dame. The 9–0–1 1948 team was runner-up to Michigan. But a national championship in 1949 would allow Notre Dame to close the decade in magnificent style.

That's exactly what happened.

Notre Dame went 10–0 in 1949, which made for a four-year mark of 36–0–2. End Leon Hart won the Heisman Trophy, and Leahy had his fourth championship and the school's seventh. Before the season, however, nobody expected a championship team to emerge from the South Bend campus. The Irish needed somebody to emerge as a leader and attention was focused on Hart, already recognized as the finest end in the college game, along with Emil Sitko, Larry Coutre, and co-captain Jim Martin.

But most observers agreed that the Fighting Irish would need more than that. Soon enough, they got it. In the sixth game of the season, against Michigan State on November 5, quarterback Bob Williams stepped to the fore. He led the top-ranked Irish to a 34–21 victory over the No. 10 Spartans in a game at East Lansing that the press thought would knock Notre Dame from its lofty perch atop collegiate football.

Williams continued to shine in subsequent games. He was at his daring best the following week in a game versus North Carolina played at Yankee Stadium. Leahy had given Williams instructions that he was never to pass the football on the fourth-down situation on their own 19-yard line, especially not with the score tied 6–6 in the second quarter.

But Williams couldn't help himself. Knowing that if he failed he'd have to head to the nearest exit to avoid Leahy, the self-assured Williams completed an 18-yard pass to Coutre for an Irish first down. Notre Dame went on to a 42–6 win, and Williams soon became recognized as the nation's best quarterback.

The Irish eased through their final two home games, rolling over Iowa 28–7 and 17th-ranked USC 32–0. All that remained was what was sure to be an easy win over Southern Methodist in Dallas. SMU would be without its top player, 1948 Heisman winner Doak Walker, and the nation had virtually conceded the national championship to Notre Dame.

Notre Dame jumped to an early lead before Mustang running back Kyle Rote came to life in the steady afternoon drizzle. Running at will, he scored two quick touchdowns and thanks to a missed extra point by SMU, the score was tied at 20 with seven minutes to go. Notre Dame's back was to the wall for the first time all season, and the offense rose to the occasion.

In blitzkrieg fashion, the Irish simply pushed SMU straight back into its own end zone with 10 determined rushes that covered 54 yards and put Notre Dame up by a touchdown, 27–20. The drive was so quick, however, that SMU still had time to score.

But in the shadow of the Notre Dame goal post, when Rote tried to pass for the tying touchdown, Notre Dame's Jerry Groom made a game-saving interception.

It was the final play of the game and of a dominating decade that saw Frank Leahy lead the Fighting Irish to three national championships in four years.

Tim Brown

Spartan Scorching Set Standard

Poor Tim Brown.

He was nervous as all get-out as he rode from New York's LaGuardia Airport to the Downtown Athletic Club. For weeks he had been thought to be the front-runner in the Heisman Trophy race, but now there seemed to be some doubt, at least if you read East Coast newspapers.

Now all of a sudden, Syracuse quarterback Don McPherson apparently had made up all kinds of ground and found traction with voters at the 11th hour. Meanwhile, Notre Dame had lost its last two regular-season games—and the college football world was finding warts on the Irish and on Brown.

Brown needn't have worried.

When the vote count hit the screen a little more than 24 hours later, it really wasn't close. Brown finished with 1,442 points—compared to 831 for McPherson and 657 for third-place Gordie Lockbaum of Holy Cross.

Brown had burst onto the scene as a junior with a scintillating season-ending performance in a come-from-behind upset of USC, then used back-to-back punt returns for touchdowns in an early-season '87 game against Michigan State to cement his Heisman bid. Listed as a flanker, Brown utilized his ability as a pass receiver, rusher out of a full-house backfield, and punt and kickoff returner to rank third nationally in all-purpose yardage as a junior (176.5 per game) and sixth as a senior (167.9).

He finished his junior campaign with 254 all-purpose yards in the 38–37 win at USC (including a 56-yard punt return that set up the winning field goal), then returned punts for 66 and 71 yards for a pair of touchdowns in an early romp over eventual Big Ten and Rose Bowl champion Michigan State.

Brown finished his career as Notre Dame's all-time leader in pass reception yards (2,493 on 137 catches) while also returning six kicks for touchdowns (three punts, three kickoffs). Despite constant double and triple coverage as a senior, he earned a reputation as the most dangerous player in college football. He benefited greatly from coach Lou Holtz's decision to create the flanker position for him, where Brown could threaten opponents as both a

The most dangerous player in college football, Tim Brown assembled 5,024 all-purpose yards and 22 touchdowns in an Irish uniform on his way to earning the 1987 Heisman Trophy.

runner (93 of his 98 career rushing attempts came in his junior and senior campaigns) and receiver. His Irish career totals included 5,024 all-purpose yards (2,493 receiving, 442 rushing, 1,613 on kickoff returns and 476 on punt returns) and 22 touchdowns.

Brown was a first-round pick of the Los Angeles Raiders (sixth player chosen overall) in the 1988 NFL draft. He was selected to play in the NFL Pro Bowl following the seasons of 1988, 1991, 1993–97, 1999–2002. He also played in his first Super Bowl in 2003. The original "Mr. Raider" signed a one-day contract with Oakland to retire as a Raider in July 2005.

A 6'0", 195-pounder from Dallas, Texas, Brown rated second-team mention (behind Anthony Carter and Johnny Rodgers) on the ABC Sports All-Time All-America team, with the following comments: "It had been 15 years since college football had seen a player create so much electricity from so many angles. Nebraska's Johnny Rodgers won the 1972 Heisman Trophy by returning punts, kickoffs, pass receptions, and handoffs into mad dashes toward the end zone. But Rodgers had very little on Notre Dame's Tim Brown. Though bigger than Rodgers, Brown was just as fast and he had the same arsenal of moves. Over his final two seasons at Notre Dame, Brown averaged 14.5 yards every time he touched the ball and an amazing 45.4 yards on 16 touchdowns. As a junior, Brown scored on kickoffs (2), receptions (5), and rushes (2). Then, two games into his senior year, Brown needed less than five minutes to return two Michigan State punts—71 yards and 66 yards—for touchdowns, the first by the Irish in 14 years."

The *Sports Illustrated* Web site, SI.com, rated Brown the ninth-greatest Irish athlete (all sports) of all time in its summer 2008 listings.

The Walter Camp Foundation selected Brown as its alumnus of the year for 2008.

27 Paul Hornung

He Could Do It All

An outstanding all-around athlete who played quarterback, left halfback, fullback, and safety, Paul Hornung remains the only player from a losing team (Notre Dame finished 2–8 in 1956) ever to win the Heisman Trophy.

As a sophomore in 1954, Hornung served as the backup fullback and also averaged 6.1 points per contest while earning a basketball monogram. As a junior, he finished fourth nationally in total offense with 1,215 yards and fifth in the Heisman voting behind Ohio State's Hopalong Cassady. Hornung ran for one score, threw for another, and intercepted two passes in a victory over fourth-ranked Navy—and then brought the Irish from behind against Iowa with a touchdown pass and game-winning field goal in the final minutes. In a loss to USC, he threw and ran for 354 yards, an NCAA high that year.

As a senior in 1956, the 6'2", 205-pounder from Louisville, Kentucky, ranked second nationally in total offense (1,337 yards), accounted for more than half the Irish scoring—and converted 67 times on either third or fourth down as a junior and senior combined.

In his 1956 Heisman-winning season, Hornung completed 59-of-111 passes for 917 yards and three touchdowns; rushed 94 times for 420 yards; caught three passes; returned four punts and 16 kickoffs; had two interceptions; and booted 14 PAT kicks. He finished with 1,066 points in the Heisman balloting—outpointing Tennessee's Johnny Majors (994) and Oklahoma's Tom McDonald (973).

Quarterback Paul Hornung won the Heisman Trophy after his prolific 1956 season where his total offense of 1,337 yards was second in the nation.

A bonus pick of the Green Bay Packers, Hornung led the NFL in scoring in 1959, '60, and '61. He retired after the 1966 season, as physical problems kept him from joining New Orleans as an expansion pick.

Hornung joined the National Football Foundation Hall of Fame in 1985 and the Pro Football Hall of Fame in 1986.

In addition to various business enterprises in Louisville, Hornung became involved in numerous television and radio ventures—including work for many years as a color commentator on Notre Dame football radio broadcasts on Westwood One.

In *The College Game* published in 1974, Hornung ranked as a first-team back in the 1950–59 college era.

The *Sports Illustrated* Web site, SI.com, rated Hornung the second-greatest Notre Dame athlete (any sport) of all time in its summer 2008 listings, declaring him "one of the most diversely talented players in Irish football history."

28 The First Game of the Century

The 1935 Ohio State Game

More than 70 years have passed since Notre Dame's unbelievable 18–13 upset of Ohio State, but the 1935 confrontation is still considered the original Game of the Century.

Although both teams were undefeated heading into the clash, the top-ranked Buckeyes were heavy favorites. One sportswriter picked Ohio State by 40 points since coach Francis "Close the Gates of Mercy" Schmidt had his Bucks riding rampant over every foe. The Irish, good but not that good, weren't given much of a chance.

But coach Elmer Layden, a former member of the Four Horsemen, said, "The 1935 team was one that believed in itself to an extraordinary extent. It was fired emotionally because death walked with it in every game."

Captain-elect Joe Sullivan, a starting tackle, had died of pneumonia several months before the season began. His teammates didn't elect another captain. Instead, they dedicated each contest to Sullivan.

Electricity had been generating in Columbus for weeks before the big game. There were parades and pep rallies. University officials and city politicians went into hiding to avoid "friends" seeking tickets. Scalpers were scoffing at any offer less than $50.

On the Friday before the game, Layden took his team to a secluded seminary outside the city for workouts, hoping to avoid the carnival-like atmosphere on campus. But when the Irish arrived, they were greeted by thousands of Buckeye fans shouting, "Catholics, go home!"

When Saturday came, more than 81,000 fans jammed into Ohio Stadium. The Buckeyes got off to a quick start and owned a commanding 13–0 lead at halftime. The pregame predictions seemed to be coming true. Ohio State's offense operated at will, and Notre Dame couldn't do anything right.

"I had never seen a Notre Dame offense so completely stopped," said writer Francis Wallace. "When the Irish passed, the ball was intercepted and converted into a touchdown. It was difficult to get a running play started against the hard-charging Ohio State line. It was even hard to get a punt away."

In the dressing room, Layden announced that the second team would start the second half. He ended his analytical pep talk by saying, "They won the first half. Now it's your turn. Go out and win this half for yourselves."

The defense finally figured out how to stop Ohio State's razzle-dazzle, and the offense, behind the superb antics of Andy Pilney, got on track. At the end of the third quarter, Ohio State was still ahead 13–0, but the Irish were driving. Notre Dame was on the Buckeyes' 12-yard line.

Pilney passed to Francis Gaul at the 2-yard line. On the next play, Steve Miller went over for the touchdown. The conversion attempt hit the crossbar and wobbled back onto the field, but Notre Dame had cracked the scoreboard.

The Irish were threatening again, but Miller fumbled in the end zone and Ohio State recovered. Notre Dame's hopes dimmed as the Bucks moved downfield. But the defense finally forced Ohio State to punt, and Notre Dame was back in the business of creating miracles.

With three minutes to go, the Irish started from their own 20-yard line. Pilney's zig-zag running brought the Irish quickly into Ohio State territory. Then he tossed a 33-yard touchdown pass to Mike Layden. A kick would tie the game. But the Irish missed again, and the Buckeyes clung to a 13–12 advantage.

Layden called for an onside kick, but Ohio State wasn't fooled and recovered the ball. All the Buckeyes had to do was maintain possession for a win. But on Dick Beltz' drive off right tackle, he was hit hard by Pilney and lost the football. Notre Dame's second-string center Henry Pojman recovered on the Ohio State 49.

The crowd was out of control. Layden sent in a play—and the ball came back to Pilney, who dropped back to throw. But all his receivers were covered. He took off, swerving to avoid a rush of Buckeye defenders. They finally forced him out of bounds on the Ohio State 19-yard line. But Pilney didn't get up. He had torn cartilage in his knee and had to be carried from the field on a stretcher.

Bill Shakespeare entered the game with half a minute remaining. He threw straight at Buckeye defender Beltz, who had his hands on the ball but couldn't hang on.

Layden sent in reserve quarterback Jim McKenna with another play. McKenna had sneaked aboard the team train to Columbus, and his teammates had helped hide him in a berth. When he could-n't scrounge up a ticket for the game, he talked his way into the Notre Dame locker room. When Layden saw him, he ordered the industrious youth to get dressed. He did, but in his excitement he forgot his pads. Now he was bringing in the winning play.

Shakespeare threw another pass. Wayne Millner caught the ball in the end zone. The miracle was almost complete.

"I've thought a lot about the pass. But I wake up nights dream-ing about the one before it—the one the Ohio State guy had in his hands and dropped," Shakespeare said years after the game. "If he'd held it, Wayne and I both would have been bums."

Pilney, the game's hero, missed the touchdown. He was being carried to the locker room.

"While they were carrying me toward the dressing room door, I was trying to turn my head, even though I was in intense pain, to see what was happening," he remembered. "I heard the crowd and the trainer says to me, 'Andy, it's over. We won.' That's the last thing I remember. Then I went out."

29 The 1946 Championship Season

The War Ends, But Irish Dominance Doesn't

World War II had finally ended, and the United States was ready to think about something more pleasant than international conflict for a change—like Notre Dame football. The year was 1946, the coach was hard-driving Frank Leahy, and it was the beginning of a dynasty for Notre Dame football.

In 1943, Leahy had guided the Fighting Irish to their first wire-service national championship, and fourth overall behind Heisman

Trophy winner Angelo Bertelli and future Heisman winner John Lujack. World War II took many football players from college, including Bertelli in the middle of his Heisman campaign in '43, but many returned to the gridiron after the war ended, including Lujack, who would go on to win the Heisman in 1947.

For the players who returned to Notre Dame in 1946, losing a college football game was not to be one of their postwar experiences. From 1946 to 1949, Notre Dame went 36–0–2 and won three national championships in one of the most successful four-year periods in college football history.

The 1946 season started it all.

Halfback Terry Brennan and linemen Bill Walsh, Bill Fischer, and John Mastrangelo were among the group of returnees from the previous season. There were several new faces who came to Notre Dame after navy hitches had interrupted their respective careers at Holy Cross and Texas A&M. There were also players for whom the war had postponed college football, like end Jim Martin and running back Emil (Red) Sitko, and there were freshmen like Leon Hart. Returning to Notre Dame along with Lujack were veterans such as tackle Zygmont (Ziggy) Czarobski, end Jack Zilly, and fullback Jim Mello. Even Leahy was coming back to Notre Dame after a couple of years in the service.

Leahy was a perfectionist and strict disciplinarian, and enduring his practices wasn't much more fun than being a soldier. But it sure produced results. The Irish usually had two separate platoons ready for each game, and often the first string didn't play much more than half the game.

On the football field, the Irish had strength in numbers, and Leahy fought a war of attrition. The season began with the Irish routing their first five opponents—Illinois, which went on to win the Western (now Big Ten) Conference championship, Pittsburgh, Purdue, Iowa, and Navy, before facing top-ranked Army. Coached by the great Earl (Red) Blaik and featuring Doc Blanchard and

Glenn Davis in the backfield, Army had won two straight national championships and 25 straight games, including two defeats of Notre Dame in the previous two seasons by a combined score of 107–0.

The showdown was set for November 9 in Yankee Stadium, where 74,121 fans turned out to see a 0–0 tie. Notre Dame advanced to the Army 4-yard line in the second quarter for the game's deepest scoring threat, but the Cadets held on downs. Blanchard broke into the clear once and appeared to be headed for a score, but an open-field tackle by Lujack saved the Irish from defeat.

Army retained its top ranking in the Associated Press poll after the game. But the Irish walloped their final three opponents by a combined score of 94–6, and were named national champions in the final poll of the season.

When the smoke cleared, the Irish found themselves the nation's statistical leaders in total offense (441.3 yards per game), rushing offense (340.1 yards per game), total defense (141.7 yards per game), and scoring defense (2.7 points per game) and had allowed only Illinois, Purdue, Iowa, and USC to score points against them.

For the season, Notre Dame outscored its opponents 271–24 in nine games.

Dan Devine

All He Did Was Win

Dan Devine was no stranger to either the college or professional football world when he came to Notre Dame. Following three seasons at Arizona State in the 1950s, 92 victories in 13 seasons at Missouri, and four years as coach of the Green Bay Packers, Devine took over the Irish in 1975.

Three seasons later he had Notre Dame once again on top of the college football world.

Devine's second season in '76 ended in a Gator Bowl win over No. 20 Penn State. The following year, the Irish dropped their second game of the '77 season at Ole Miss. A week later, quarterback Joe Montana came off the bench in an epic comeback win at Purdue—and he never left the starting lineup again.

In a critical midseason home game against fifth-ranked USC and in one of the most memorable scenes in the history of Notre Dame Stadium, Notre Dame's team emerged wearing green jerseys. That served as one of the catalysts in a 49–19 Irish victory that day.

The fifth-ranked and once-beaten Irish earned an eventual Cotton Bowl berth against undefeated and top-rated Texas—and a historic defensive effort against Heisman winner Earl Campbell

Coach Dan Devine knew how to win and was inducted into the College Football Hall of Fame in 1985.

helped Notre Dame knock off the Longhorns 38–10. That propelled the Irish from fifth to first in the final polls and earned Devine and his Irish Notre Dame's 10th consensus national championship.

A year later, the Irish won eight straight regular-season games, including victories over ranked opponents Pittsburgh, Navy, and Georgia Tech. That sent 10th-ranked Notre Dame back to the Cotton Bowl to meet Southwest Conference champ Houston. In the ice and cold of Dallas, it was Montana who generated a miracle comeback, as the Irish overcame a 34–12 deficit with Montana throwing the game-winning touchdown pass as time ran out.

Devine announced his retirement prior to the 1980 season— then a week into that campaign Harry Oliver's record 51-yard field goal enabled the Irish to defeat Michigan. Unbeaten Notre Dame rose to No. 1 in the nation by November, shut out fifth-ranked Alabama in Birmingham to cinch a Sugar Bowl invitation, then barely missed out in a 17–10 loss to top-rated Georgia and Herschel Walker in New Orleans in what would be Devine's final game as a head coach.

Devine coached an Outland Trophy winner in Ross Browner in 1976—and a year later Browner won both the Lombardi and Maxwell awards. He also coached the '77 Walter Camp player of the year in Ken MacAfee, as well as consensus All-Americans Luther Bradley, Browner, Bob Crable, Vagas Ferguson, Bob Golic, Dave Huffman, MacAfee, Steve Niehaus, and John Scully. During his tenure in South Bend, Jerome Heavens in '78 and then Ferguson in '79 became Notre Dame's all-time leading groundgainers.

Five years after his retirement, Devine was selected to the College Football Hall of Fame. His tenure at Missouri (1958–70) made him part of the only string of three coaches at an institution that all made the Hall of Fame—the other Tiger coaches being Don Faurot (1935–42, 1946–56) and Frank Broyles (1957). He's also one of the links at two other schools with consecutive Hall of Fame coaches—with Ara Parseghian (1964–74) at Notre Dame, and with Frank Kush (1958–79) at Arizona State.

John Lattner

Was There Anything He Couldn't Do?

John Lattner claimed the Heisman Trophy in 1953 during his senior year—in the second-closest Heisman balloting in history—despite the fact he didn't lead the Irish in rushing, passing, receiving, or scoring.

A jack of all trades who barely nosed out Minnesota's Paul Giel for the award (Lattner had 1,850 points to 1,794 for Giel), Lattner benefited from helping Leahy's final Notre Dame team to a 9–0–1 record that earned the Irish national title recognition from all selectors but the two wire services (they named unbeaten Maryland). Lattner received the Maxwell Award as the top collegiate player as both a junior and senior and finished fifth in the Heisman voting as a junior behind Oklahoma's Billy Vessels.

A consensus All-American as both a junior and senior on offense and defense, the 6'1", 190-pounder from Chicago made his mark by running, catching, and punting the football, while also returning punts and kickoffs and intercepting 13 career passes. He established a record for all-purpose yards from rushing, receiving, and runbacks—a mark that stood until Vagas Ferguson broke it in 1979. He finished with 321 kickoff return yards on only eight returns (two for touchdowns) as a senior.

His Heisman-winning season in 1953 also included 651 rushing yards (and nine touchdowns), 204 receiving yards (on 14 catches), 103 punt-return yards, and four interceptions.

ESPN's Beano Cook rates Lattner as his best-ever defensive back. In its 2008 title *The College Football Book, Sports Illustrated* named him a second-team back on its 1950s all-decade squad.

Lattner played one year with the Pittsburgh Steelers before entering the service and suffering a career-ending knee injury in a military game. A former restaurant owner in Chicago, he became an executive for a business forms company.

Lattner was elected to the National Football Foundation Hall of Fame in 1979.

32 The 1929 Championship Season

First of a Pair for the Irish

If the Great Depression wasn't reason enough for Notre Dame football partisans to be a little down, then the fact the Irish were without a home for the 1929 season was surely enough to bring some anxiety into the minds of both the team and its followers. Plans were underway at Notre Dame for a new stadium to be built, and '29 was the transition year in which the Irish had no home facility.

That didn't keep Notre Dame from winning, however, something the team had accomplished only five times in nine tries in 1928. Knute Rockne had promised to return Notre Dame football in '29 to what had become its customary level of excellence, home-field advantage or not. And he would not be stopped from fulfilling that promise.

The closest the Irish came to having a home game in '29 were three games contested at Soldier Field in Chicago. The Irish defeated Wisconsin there 19–0 on October 19, then Drake 19–7 on November 9, and finally USC in the most important game of the year, 13–12, before 112,912 fans on November 16.

The lack of home turf was not the only major difficulty of the '29 season for Notre Dame. The team's legendary coach was battling phlebitis, which doctors said stood a 50–50 chance of taking Rockne's life if he tried to coach that season. But coach the team he did through one dramatic victory after another, either by telephone from a hospital bed or from a wheelchair on the sidelines.

An announcement was made that Rockne would not accompany the team on its trip to Baltimore to face Navy. Line coach Tom Lieb took over for Rockne that day, as the Irish won 14–7. But back in South Bend, doctor's orders couldn't keep Rock away from practice at Cartier Field, where he set up his command post in his car and used a loudspeaker to direct activities.

By the time the USC contest rolled around, the Irish were 6–0 and recognized as one of the top teams in the nation. Running back Joe Savoldi had earned acclaim in the Wisconsin game with dazzling touchdown runs of 71 and 40 yards, and he provided the only score of the game in Notre Dame's 7–0 win at Carnegie Tech on October 26.

When the Irish faced USC at Soldier Field, Rockne's status was as bad as ever, but the team needed him. The Notre Dame–USC tradition was already a great one, and the first half foretold the kind of game everyone expected, with the teams battling to a 6–6 tie.

In the locker room, the Fighting Irish were in desperate need of one of Rock's famous speeches, but he was nowhere to be found. So former Irish running back Paul Castner stepped up to do what he could, and in the middle of his oration, who should two Irish managers wheel into the room but Rockne himself. He was in great pain and had undergone quite a strain—not only from making the trip to Chicago but also from watching his team struggle in the first half.

He gave an impassioned speech with what strength he had, during which a blood clot in one leg broke loose, passed through his heart and settled safely in the other leg. His speech worked, as the Irish escaped Chicago with a 13–12 win and an unblemished 7–0 record.

The Irish still had traditional foes Northwestern and Army left. Northwestern fell relatively easy, as the Irish posted a win on the Wildcats' home field. But the November 30 matchup with Army at Yankee Stadium proved to be a real battle.

The game was played on turf that was frozen solid, and neither team was able to accomplish anything. It was eight degrees at game time and a biting wind cut across the field as the players dashed out for the opening kickoff.

The first quarter was scoreless, but in the second period Army drove deep into Irish territory. When Red Cagle lofted a pass for end Carl Carlmark, it looked like a certain score for the Cadets. But Notre Dame's Jack Elder came out of nowhere to snatch the ball away. He took it 96 yards for the game's only touchdown. The extra point was added to make it 7–0 Irish, and that's the way it stayed. Notre Dame ended up 9–0 and the season was over. The team had survived without a home, Rockne had survived his illness, and Notre Dame had its second consensus national championship.

33 1946–49 Under Leahy

Four Seasons, No Defeats

Notre Dame's 1950 graduating class had the unique pleasure of never seeing its football team lose a game.

In fact, *Sports Illustrated* listed those Irish football teams of 1946–49 as the No. 2 sports dynasty of the twentieth century, trailing only the 1957–69 Boston Celtics who won 11 NBA titles in a

In four seasons under Leahy's strict discipline, Notre Dame went 36–0–2, won three national titles, and had two Heisman Trophy winners.

13-year span and featured the likes of Bill Russell, Bob Cousy, and coach Red Auerbach.

The magazine's tribute to the Irish dynasty of 1946–49 read as follows (*Sports Illustrated* also published an extensive article about those 1946–49 Notre Dame teams by Paul Zimmerman), "Only one team could match up with Notre Dame in the years after World War II: the Irish second string. In four seasons under coach Frank Leahy, Notre Dame went 36–0–2, won three national titles, and had two Heisman Trophy winners [Johnny Lujack in 1947, and Leon Hart in '49]."

Other top dynasties on the list included UCLA basketball, with 10 NCAA titles in a 12-year stretch, from 1964–75…but three losses to the Irish during that stretch, including the end to the Bruins' NCAA-record 88-game winning streak on January 19, 1974; the 1947–1962 New York Yankees (10 World Series titles in a 16-year span); and the 1991–98 Chicago Bulls (six NBA titles).

Notre Dame athletics has ties to other dynasties on the list as well. No. 9 North Carolina women's soccer (1979–99) posted a 442–17–11 record during that period, with one of those losses coming to Notre Dame in the 1995 NCAA semifinals (plus a tie in '94 that ended Carolina's NCAA-record 92-game winning streak); No. 10 Oklahoma football (1953–57) won a still-standing NCAA-record 47 consecutive games and back-to-back national titles during that time, with that 47-game streak stopped by Notre Dame in Norman on November 16, 1957, (7–0); and the No. 15 Green Bay Packers (1961–67) featured former Notre Dame quarterback Paul Hornung in 1961–62.

The College Game in 1974 listed end Leon Hart, tackle George Connor, guard Bill Fischer, and back John Lujack as first-teamers in the 1940–49 period.

During those four combined seasons of 1946–49, Notre Dame won three consensus national titles, produced a pair of Heisman Trophy winners, and 17 first-team All-Americans—defeating eight ranked opponents in that period. The '46 team led the country in total offense, rushing, total defense, and scoring defense. The '49 squad also led the nation in total offense. All four squads rated fourth or better nationally in rushing and seventh or better in scoring.

34 John Huarte

From Nowhere to the Heisman

John Huarte's 1964 Heisman Trophy storybook victory ranks as one of the biggest upsets in the history of the award, considering he

In 1964, quarterback John Huarte posted a textbook season to set 12 school records and win the Heisman Trophy.

missed much of his sophomore season due to injury and didn't even play enough as a junior to win a monogram.

Behind the aerial efforts of Huarte and fellow Californian Jack Snow (who caught 60 passes that year for 1,114 yards and a record nine touchdowns), Ara Parseghian in his first year turned Notre Dame from a 2–7 team in 1963 into a 9–1 squad that in '64 came within minutes of the national title. Huarte threw for 270 yards in the '64 opening-game upset of Wisconsin—including touchdown tosses of 61 and 42 yards to Snow—and ended up finishing the year ranked third nationally in total offense (2,069 yards). He set 12 Irish records that year and also earned back-of-the-year and player-of-the-year honors from United Press International.

The 6'0", 180-pounder from Santa Ana, California, received 1,026 points in the Heisman balloting, placing ahead of Tulsa's

Jerry Rhome (952) and Illinois linebacker Dick Butkus (505). Snow finished fifth with 187 points.

Huarte's senior numbers featured 114 completions on 205 pass attempts for 2,062 yards and 16 touchdowns. He rushed for another three scores.

A second-round draft pick of the New York Jets, Huarte played sparingly in the pro ranks for eight years with Boston, Philadelphia, Kansas City, and Chicago—prior to retiring from the World Football League Memphis entry in 1975.

Huarte was inducted into the College Football Hall of Fame in 2005.

35 Ending the Longest Win Streak Ever

The 1957 Oklahoma Game

The odds were stacked heavily against the Irish.

The 1957 Sooners, defending national champions and No. 2 in the weekly polls, boasted the country's longest winning streak at 47 games. Oklahoma had not lost since the 1953 home opener when Notre Dame ruined the Sooners' season debut, 28–21.

Powerful Oklahoma, which had blasted the Irish 40–0 the year before in South Bend, had scored in 123 consecutive contests and was averaging 300 yards a game. The Sooners, playing in their own massive stadium in Norman, Oklahoma, were favored by at least 19 points.

Notre Dame, which suffered through its first losing season in 23 years in 1956, had dropped two straight to Navy and Michigan State (the Irish were outscored 54–12 in those two contests). Coach Terry Brennan was under fire.

Although the Sooners moved all the way down to the Irish 13-yard line on their first possession, the Notre Dame defense dug in and held. Oklahoma would get no closer the rest of the afternoon. Both teams threatened with several offensive drives, but strong defensive stands keep the score at a standstill until late in the fourth quarter.

"I was willing to settle for a scoreless tie in the third quarter," admitted Oklahoma coach Bud Wilkinson. "I felt at the start of the second half we had a good chance. But after we couldn't get going, even with our tremendous punting to their goal, I was ready to settle for a scoreless tie."

The Irish, however, had other plans. With 3:50 left in the game, Notre Dame needed three yards on fourth down to cross the goal line. Quarterback Bob Williams, who had executed nearly every play perfectly all afternoon, faked to Nick Pietrosante in the middle and then pitched to halfback Dick Lynch. Lynch went wide around right end for the touchdown, Monty Stickles kicked the extra point, and Notre Dame had its 7–0 upset.

Williams, who engineered the 80-yard drive in 20 plays, explained, "They were in tight, real tight, just waiting for me to give the ball to Pietrosante. Well, I just faked to him and tossed out to Lynch and it worked like a charm."

Coach Brennan, who often called the victory the "greatest thrill of my athletic career," credited the defense with the win.

"We prepared for them in detail," Brennan said. "We didn't have a whole lot of speed and we tried to be as basic as possible. There were only four or five basic plays—and if you stopped them you had a chance to win. The big thing was to stop their running game."

The Irish indeed halted the Sooners' ground attack. Oklahoma managed just 98 yards rushing.

When the team arrived back in South Bend after the victory, the Irish were met by more than 5,000 fans. That hearty welcome was richly deserved as Oklahoma's 47-game winning streak remains the longest in college football.

36 Angelo Bertelli

Even a War Can't Stop Heisman Run

Frank Leahy's switch to the T-formation starting in 1942 made a star of Angelo Bertelli and helped him win the 1943 Heisman Trophy as a senior despite playing in only six of Notre Dame's 10 games.

Bertelli's Irish career began as a singlewing tailback in 1941 as his 1,027 passing yards (and a .569 completion percentage that led the nation) propelled his team to a 9–0–1 record. As a junior, he switched to quarterback in the T and ended up throwing for another 1,039 yards and 10 touchdowns. In a 27–0 win over

After an impressive Notre Dame career, Angelo Bertelli won the 1943 Heisman Trophy. He played in just six of his senior season's 10 games because he was called to service in the Marines.

Stanford that year, he threw four touchdown passes and completed a record 10 straight passes.

Runner-up to Minnesota's Bruce Smith for the Heisman as a sophomore and sixth as a junior behind winner Frank Sinkwich of Georgia, Bertelli's play enabled Notre Dame to average 43.5 points in its first six games in 1943 before the Marine Corps called him into service. Still, he threw 10 scoring passes in those six contests and helped Notre Dame claim the national title despite a final-game loss to Great Lakes while Bertelli was in boot camp.

A 6'1", 173-pounder from Springfield, Massachusetts, Bertelli played three seasons with Los Angeles and Chicago in the All-America Football Conference before a knee injury ended his career. After that, Bertelli ran a beverage distributorship in Clifton, New Jersey.

Bertelli was rated a second-team back on the 1940s all-decade team in the 2008 *Sports Illustrated* book, *The College Football Book*.

He joined the National Football Foundation College Football Hall of Fame in 1972. Bertelli died on June 26, 1999.

37 The 1966 Championship Season

An Irish Defense for the Ages

In his third season at Notre Dame, coach Ara Parseghian made a difficult decision at the start of the 1966 season and selected sophomore Terry Hanratty as his starting quarterback over classmate Coley O'Brien. Yet the decision proved without a doubt to be the correct one, as Hanratty and sophomore split end Jim Seymour turned out to be one of the best passing combinations Notre Dame fans have ever seen.

The two had begun working together during the previous winter, developing their timing, moves, and patterns so they would know each other's habits inside out when the '66 season began. Seymour was a good bet to take over one of the end positions that was being vacated after the '65 season, but Hanratty had no such assurances of whether or not he would be the No. 1 quarterback.

Fortunately for Hanratty, Parseghian decided to balance an already steady running game, manned by Nick Eddy, Larry Conjar, and Rocky Bleier, with the passing talent of Hanratty. The decision bore fruit in the first game of the season, as Hanratty and Seymour hooked up 13 times for 276 yards—Notre Dame records for receptions and yards—and three touchdowns, which tied a school record. The Irish defeated Rose Bowl–bound Purdue that day, 26–14, in South Bend.

Notre Dame traveled to Northwestern for the second game of the season and won 35–7. The Irish defense gave up its last points for the next three games and showed the kind of determination that ensured Notre Dame would never be out of any contest. Notre Dame returned home for the next two games and defeated Army and North Carolina by a combined score of 67–0, setting the stage for a showdown with Oklahoma.

Notre Dame traveled to Norman for what was supposed to be anybody's ballgame. The game was billed as a matchup between the small, quick, strong Sooners and the big, slow Irish. But 10th-ranked Oklahoma was out of its depth. Although the Irish lost Seymour to an ankle injury that would cost him two games, the Fighting Irish rolled to a 38–0 victory and their third straight shutout of the young season.

Notre Dame pounded its next three opponents—Navy, Pittsburgh, and Duke—giving up only one score, a touchdown to Navy. Meanwhile, the offense was hitting on all cylinders, racking up 31 points versus the Midshipmen, 40 against Pitt, and a whopping 64 against the Blue Devils.

The game of the century took place on November 19 when No. 1 Notre Dame traveled to East Lansing, Michigan, to play second-ranked Michigan State for all the marbles. Notre Dame fell behind 10–0 in the second quarter, but O'Brien, who had been diagnosed with diabetes only a few weeks earlier and was still adjusting, brought the Irish back to a tie in the second half. The Spartan offense was unable to net a single yard running the ball in the second half, and when Notre Dame intercepted a pass and returned it to the Spartan 18-yard line in the fourth quarter, it looked like Notre Dame's chance to win. Three plays for minus-six yards left the Irish with a 41-yard field goal attempt, which sailed wide to the right.

Notre Dame had the ball again on its own 30 with 1:24 left in the game. But rather than gamble with passes deep in their own territory, the Irish attempted to run the ball out of danger. The game was a 10–10 tie.

The Irish held on to their top ranking and traveled to Los Angeles to play Rose Bowl–bound USC. The Irish tore the Trojans apart, 51–0, posting the team's sixth shutout in 10 games and ensuring another unanimous number-one selection for the national championship.

In the recent book, *Fifty Years of College Football*, the '66 Notre Dame squad (9–0–1) was rated the ninth-greatest team in college football since 1955.

38 The 1988 Championship Season

No One Proved Better

It wasn't long after Lou Holtz's arrival as head football coach at Notre Dame that he opined that the Irish couldn't expect to be a great team until they were great on defense.

That prophesy came true for Holtz and the Irish in 1988—ironically, just a year after Notre Dame's Tim Brown had captured the Heisman Trophy. But with his departure came a revitalization of the defense led by senior defensive end Frank Stams, junior linebacker Michael Stonebreaker, sophomore defensive tackle Chris Zorich, and senior linebacker Wes Pritchett, all of whom merited some sort of All-America honors (as did offensive tackle and captain Andy Heck). They were supported by cornerback Todd Lyght, linebacker Ned Bolcar, and defensive tackle Jeff Alm, who went on to earn that same All-America acclaim a year later.

The end result was a consensus national championship for the Irish in 1988, thanks to a perfect 12–0 campaign. The title came in Holtz's third season as Irish head coach, much as Frank Leahy, Ara Parseghian, and Dan Devine before him had claimed national crowns in their respective third seasons as Irish head coach. It came thanks to riveting regular-season triumphs over Michigan, Miami, and USC—and it ultimately featured wins over teams ranked first, second, and third in the polls when they faced Notre Dame.

When the 13th-ranked Irish debuted against ninth-rated Michigan in Notre Dame Stadium, Holtz knew his youthful offense would be tested, particularly with a green group of receivers featuring Ricky Watters at flanker in a switch from tailback, plus rookies Derek Brown and Raghib Ismail. His concern appeared legit when Notre Dame did not score a touchdown from scrimmage.

But Watters returned a Michigan punt 81 yards for a touchdown, and unheralded walk-on kicker Reggie Ho knocked through four field goals, twice bringing the Irish from behind—including the game winner with 1:13 remaining. A field goal miss by the Wolverines from 48 yards as time expired earned Notre Dame a 19–17 opening victory.

Four wins later, the fourth-rated Irish welcomed top-ranked Miami and its 36-game regular-season unbeaten streak to Notre

Dame Stadium. The streak bit the dust that day by a 31–30 count, as Notre Dame forced seven Hurricane turnovers and made use of a bevy of heroes, lastly Pat Terrell, who knocked down Miami quarterback Steve Walsh's two-point conversion pass with 45 seconds remaining.

Terrell previously ran an interception back 60 yards for a score, Stams forced two Walsh fumbles, recovered another, and tipped the pass Terrell intercepted—and quarterback Tony Rice threw for a then-career-high 195 yards. The Irish took the lead for good midway through the third period after thwarting a fake punt by Miami and then held on down the stretch. Though Walsh threw for 424 yards, the stingy Irish front line limited the 'Canes to 57 rushing yards.

The season finale found the 10–0 and top-ranked Irish underdogs against second-rated and also unbeaten USC in the Los Angeles Coliseum. Again, it was defense that dominated for Notre Dame in a 27–10 victory. Stams had nine tackles, two-and-a-half sacks, a fumble recovery, and he made life miserable for Trojan standout Rodney Peete. Cornerback Stan Smagala ran an interception back 64 yards for a 20–7 halftime lead after Rice had skirted left end for 65 yards for the first points of the game.

The Irish prevailed despite going 29 minutes in the second and third periods combined without a first down—and in spite of the fact that leading rusher Tony Brooks and leading receiver Watters, both sophomores, were suspended the day before the game.

Notre Dame met third-ranked and unbeaten West Virginia in the Fiesta Bowl in hopes of claiming the championship—and the Irish rode early leads of 16–0 and 23–3 to an eventual 34–21 victory banking on another staunch defensive effort.

Rice ran for 75 yards and completed seven throws for 213 more yards. Meanwhile, Stams had two sacks on his way to the defensive MVP award, and the Irish dominated a heralded Mountaineer offensive line that had been one of the main reasons West Virginia had never trailed in a game all season.

Just as it had beat up USC's Peete, the more physical Notre Dame team knocked quarterback Major Harris out of the contest early with a bruised shoulder and limited the potent Mountaineer ground game to 108 yards.

The Irish finished third nationally in scoring defense (12.3 points per game)—and 22 of the 24 starters were eventually drafted by NFL squads.

Holtz's final pronouncement: "This team will go down as a great football team because nobody proved otherwise. If we are number one, I don't care who is number two."

39 The 1977 Championship Season

The "Greening" of the Irish

Who could forget the cover of *Sports Illustrated* the week after Notre Dame had defeated top-rated Texas 38–10 in the 1978 Cotton Bowl? A fierce Terry Eurick was pictured fighting through a hole in the offensive line, the caption reading, "The Irish Wake the Echoes."

On the inside, "Shakin' Down the Thunder" was the title of an article about how Notre Dame's victory over the previously unbeaten Longhorns was enough to vault the Irish from fifth to first in the wire-service polls and give the university its seventh wire-service national championship and 10th overall.

The theme for that January 2 matchup in Dallas could have been "and then there were none." For there was not one unbeaten team remaining after the Irish had knocked Texas from its No. 1 ranking. Third-year Irish coach Dan Devine made sure his charges were ready to take care of America's last undefeated team.

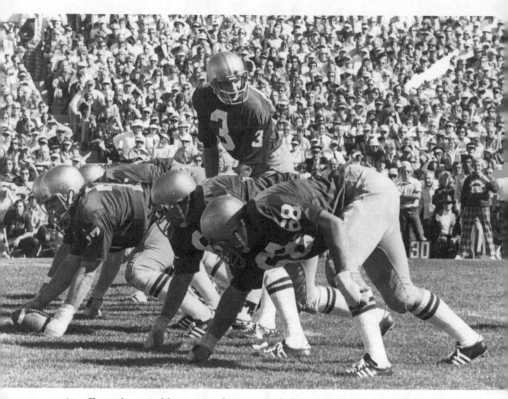

An offense that would not quit characterized the 1977 team led by quarterback Joe Montana, running back Jerome Heavens, and All-American tight end Ken MacAfee.

An unrelenting defense was the reason why. The defense featured 1976 Outland Trophy winner Ross Browner at one end and Willie Fry at the other, supported by a tough, mobile group of linebackers headed by All-American Bob Golic.

The Irish forced six Texas turnovers in the Cotton Bowl, and an opportunistic offense capitalized on five of them. Notre Dame's devastating strength in the trenches roped up Texas' Heisman Trophy winner Earl Campbell. He managed a tough 116 yards on 29 carries.

Notre Dame's defensive strength came as no surprise in 1977, and it was the primary reason the Irish were near the top of the polls in the preseason rankings. But it was an unexpected boost from the offense that gave Notre Dame the national championship in '77.

Quarterback Joe Montana and running back Jerome Heavens both rebounded on offense, teaming with All-American tight end Ken MacAfee, who led the team in receiving for the third straight year.

The offense came on strong in '77 as Montana threw for more than 1,600 yards and 11 touchdowns and Heavens led the team with 994 rushing yards. Montana earned a reputation as "The Comeback Kid" with performances like the one he had in the third game of the season when, in his first appearance in more than a year, he engineered the Irish to 17 fourth-quarter points in Notre Dame's come-from-behind 31–24 win at Purdue.

Later in the season, the Irish traveled to Death Valley to play the 15th-ranked Clemson Tigers, and Montana scored two fourth-quarter touchdowns to bring the Irish to a 21–17 win.

Heavens proved himself with 136 yards against Michigan State and followed his outburst against the Spartans with a Notre Dame–record 200 yards rushing versus Army. Two weeks later he went for 100 against Navy.

But the key regular season win came in a mid-season 49–19 thrashing of fifth-ranked USC in Notre Dame Stadium. In that one, the Irish warmed up in their usual blue jerseys, only to emerge in green just prior to kickoff. That triumph helped wipe out the memory of Notre Dame's second-game road loss, a 20–13 defeat at Ole Miss that proved its sole '77 blemish.

The Irish ran out to a 24–10 halftime lead in the Cotton Bowl and then added touchdowns in each of the final quarters for an overwhelming 28-point victory. Few questioned who was No. 1.

"I don't like to say it was easy, but…well, the way we played today, we could have dominated any line in the country," said Irish offensive tackle Tim Foley on the Irish win over Texas.

"At least the team that beat us was a good one. Everyone can't say that," said Texas coach Fred Akers.

Notre Dame leapfrogged over the four teams ranked ahead of it to grab the nation's top position. Only one time in history (Wisconsin from No. 8 to No. 1 in 1952) did a team make a bigger AP jump into the top slot. The Irish did, indeed, wake the echoes and shake down the thunder.

The Irish that season ranked in the national top 10 in three statistical categories—fifth in total offense (440.0 yards per game), seventh in scoring (34.7), and third in rushing defense (89.2).

40 Academics

Irish Dominate These Rankings, Too

The University of Notre Dame ranked No. 1 in the country in terms of graduating its student-athletes, according to the latest NCAA statistics released in the fall of 2008.

Whether measured by the federal government in its Department of Education report or by the NCAA through its newer Graduation Success Rate (GSR) numbers, graduation rates for Notre Dame student-athletes also rank among the national leaders in all major categories among all major football–playing colleges and universities.

Notre Dame led the nation in the 2008 GSR ratings for all student-athletes (at 98, tied with the U.S. Naval Academy), while also ranking first in both the GSR and federal standings for female student-athletes (100 GSR, 93 federal)—as well as first in the federal listing for black student-athletes (84). Both the federal graduation-rate figures and the GSR numbers for Notre Dame student-athletes found the Irish ranked fourth or better nationally in five major categories among the 119 football-playing institutions in the NCAA Football Bowl Subdivision (formerly Division I-A).

The federally mandated NCAA Graduation-Rates Report, the 18th such survey issued by the association, covered students who enrolled between 1998 and 2001 at all Division I institutions. The federal graduation rates are based on the raw percentage of student-athletes who entered an institution and graduated within six years. Students who leave or transfer, regardless of academic standing, are considered non-graduates. All those receiving athletic aid are included in the statistics. All military academies are exempt from the federal survey because they do not offer grants-in-aid to student-athletes.

The GSR was created to more accurately reflect actual graduation rates by including transfer data in the calculation. College and university presidents asked the NCAA to develop a new methodology that takes into account the mobility among students in today's higher education environment. Research indicates that approximately 60 percent of all new bachelor's degree recipients attend more than one undergraduate institution during their collegiate careers.

In calculations listing all student-athletes in all sports, Notre Dame tied for first among the Bowl Subdivision football schools in the GSR figures, which were initiated in 2005 by the NCAA. The University's 98 percent GSR for all its student-athletes matched that for the U.S. Naval Academy. Using the federal formula, Notre Dame graduated a four-year average of 89 percent of its student-athletes, just behind Stanford at 91 percent.

Notre Dame graduated 93 percent of all women competing in varsity athletics to rank first among its peer institutions (tied with Northwestern) based on the federal calculations. Among men, Notre Dame's 87-percent federal rate was second behind Stanford's 90-percent rate.

Notre Dame graduated 84 percent of its black student-athletes, ranking first nationally based on the federal rate, and Irish football players graduated at an 85-percent rate, to rank fourth. In the GSR standings, in addition to its No. 1 ranking for all student-athletes, Notre Dame finished tied for first among female student athletes at 100 (Vanderbilt and the U.S. Naval Academy also finished at 100), second among male student-athletes at 97 percent (behind the Naval Academy at 98), second among football players at 94 percent (behind the Naval Academy at 95), and second among black student-athletes at 96 percent (behind the Naval Academy at 98).

The NCAA also calculated graduation rates over a 10-year period (student-athletes who entered from 1992–93 through 2001–02). During those 10 years, Notre Dame had 627 student-athletes who exhausted their eligibility—and 100 percent of them graduated within the allotted six-year period. By comparison, Northwestern had a 100-percent rate, Duke recorded 99 percent, and Boston College and Stanford both had 98 percent rates.

Nine of Notre Dame's athletic programs posted federal graduation rates of 100 percent. The federal figures showed that—among Notre Dame's men's sports—fencing, lacrosse, and swimming and diving achieved 100-percent scores. Cross country/track and field scored 95, soccer scored 94, tennis 93, and hockey 92 (good for first place).

Among the Irish women's programs, cross country/track and field, fencing, golf, lacrosse, rowing, and tennis all posted 100 scores. Swimming and diving scored 96 (good for first), and volleyball scored 91.

Notre Dame ranked second among the NCAA FBS (formerly Division I-A) football-playing institutions in 100 scores with its nine. Stanford had 11, Duke eight—and Northwestern seven.

Eleven Irish programs had federal rates that ranked them first within their sport among the NCAA FBS subset of 119 schools, while four other programs finished among the top seven:

- Men's lacrosse finished by itself in first place with its 100 score.
- Men's fencing at 100 tied for first with Penn State, Rutgers, and Stanford.
- Men's swimming at 100 tied for first with Maryland, Miami (Florida), and Rice.
- Women's cross country/track and field at 100 tied for first with Duke.
- Women's fencing at 100 tied for first with Northwestern and Penn State.
- Women's golf at 100 tied for first with 15 other schools.
- Women's lacrosse at 100 tied for first with Boston College, California, Duke, Penn State, Stanford, and Virginia.
- Women's rowing at 100 tied for first with Duke, Indiana, Minnesota, and North Carolina.
- Women's tennis at 100 tied for first with 19 other schools.
- Hockey at 92 ranked first—followed by Miami (Ohio) at 69, Boston College (68), and Michigan (65).
- Women's swimming at 96 finished tied for first with Iowa State.
- Men's soccer at 94 ranked tied for fourth (with Purdue), behind Duke, Stanford, and Virginia Tech (all at 100).
- Football at 85 tied for fourth with Vanderbilt, behind Stanford (89), Boston College (88), and Duke (86).
- Baseball at 80 ranked sixth behind Boston College (100), Northwestern (96), Stanford (91), Michigan (88), and Buffalo (81).
- Men's cross country/track and field at 95 ranked seventh— behind Duke, SMU, Miami (Florida), New Mexico State, Stanford, and Wake Forest (all at 100).

Nineteen of 22 athletics programs at Notre Dame compiled GSR rates of 100 percent, and none were below 90 percent according to the fourth year of the GSR measurements developed by the NCAA.

None of the 119 FBS programs in the country had a higher percentage of 100 GSR scores than did Notre Dame with its .863 figure (19-of-22). That marked the third time in the four years of the survey that Notre Dame ranked number one in percentage of teams with 100 scores.

Here are the top 10 in that category (these are the only 10 institutions with 50 or more percent of their sports registering 100 marks):

Institution	Percentage	100 Scores/Sports Rated
1. Notre Dame	.863	19/22
2. Northwestern	.789	15/19
3. Boston College	.740	20/27
4. Duke	.681	15/22
5. Vanderbilt	.667	8/12
6. Wake Forest	.642	9/14
7. Stanford	.629	17/27
8. U.S. Naval Academy	.578	11/19
9. Rice	.539	7/13
10. Tulane	.500	6/12

The NCAA figures showed that all 11 Irish women's programs posted a GSR of 100 percent—basketball, cross country/track, fencing, golf, lacrosse, rowing, soccer, softball, swimming, tennis, and volleyball.

Among Notre Dame's men's sports, baseball, basketball, cross country/track, fencing, lacrosse, soccer, swimming, and tennis achieved 100-percent GSR scores. Ice hockey scored 96 percent, football scored 94 percent, and golf was 90.

Overall, that's one more perfect score in 2008 than in 2007 for the Irish programs, after Notre Dame recorded 18 100-percent GSR scores (of 22 sports) in 2007.

In 2005, among the 119 NCAA Division I-A football-playing institutions, Notre Dame had the highest percentage of its sports with 100-percent scores, with a .800 figure (16-of-20). The 2006 data put Notre Dame's percentage at .773 (17-of-22), to rank second behind the U.S. Naval Academy. The 2007 data put Notre Dame's percentage at .818 (18-of-22), which again ranked No. 1.

The 2008 national GSR for Division I-A was 78 percent, up from 77 in 2007 and in 2006 (and up one percent from the 76 figure in 2005).

Notre Dame programs again rank among the best in the country based on 2008 GSR figures—including first-place or second-place ratings in the sports of football, men's basketball and women's basketball.

In football, Notre Dame achieved a 94 GSR rating in 2008, with only the U.S. Naval Academy (at 95) ranking higher among FBS schools.

Here are the FBS institutions with scores of 80 or higher in that category:

Score	Institution
95	U.S. Naval Academy
94	Notre Dame
93	Stanford
92	Boston College, Duke, Northwestern
91	Vanderbilt
90	U.S. Air Force Academy
87	U.S. Military Academy
83	Miami (Ohio), Wake Forest
82	Rice
81	Ohio University
80	Southern Mississippi

In men's basketball, Notre Dame achieved a perfect 100 GSR rating, with only Bowling Green, Florida State, Utah State, and Wake Forest also reaching the top slot.

Here are the FBS institutions with scores of 80 or higher in that category:

Score	Institution
100	Bowling Green, Florida State, Notre Dame, Utah State, Wake Forest
97	U.S. Naval Academy, U.S. Military Academy
92	Oklahoma State
91	BYU, Marshall, U.S. Air Force Academy
90	Northwestern
89	Duke, Florida
86	North Carolina, Wisconsin
83	Colorado State, Rice, SMU
82	Alabama, Northern Illinois
80	Hawaii, Illinois, Ohio University, Troy, Vanderbilt

In women's basketball, Notre Dame also achieved a 100 GSR rating, as one of 26 Division I-A football-playing institutions with a perfect score.

Here are the FBS institutions with scores of 90 or higher in that category:

Score	Institution
100	Boise State, Boston College, BYU, UCLA, Clemson, Colorado, Connecticut, Florida, Kent State, Miami (Fla.), Nebraska, Northwestern, Notre Dame, Ohio State, Oregon State, Rice, Stanford, Syracuse, Tennessee, Texas, Toledo, Tulane, U.S. Naval Academy, Vanderbilt, Wake Forest, Washington

98	U.S. Military Academy
95	Ball State
93	Bowling Green, Colorado State, Iowa State, Memphis, Miami (Ohio), Nevada, Oregon, Pittsburgh, Wyoming
92	Arkansas, Central Florida, East Carolina, Idaho, Illinois, Iowa, Penn State, SMU, Virginia Tech
91	Buffalo, Washington State
90	Arizona State, Duke, Indiana, Kentucky, North Carolina

Here's a summary of how Notre Dame fared in both federal and GSR comparisons in a handful of categories:

2008 NCAA Graduation Rates
All data for student-athletes who enrolled between 1998–2001 (numbers are percentages)

All Student-Athletes

Federal Rate	*GSR*
1. Stanford, 91	1. Notre Dame, 98
2. Notre Dame, 89	(tie) U.S. Naval Academy, 98
3. Duke, 88	3. Northwestern, 97
(tie) Northwestern, 88	(tie) Duke, 97
5. Boston College, 85	5. Boston College, 96
6. Penn State, 82	6. Stanford, 95
7. Vanderbilt, 79	7. Vanderbilt, 94
(tie) Rice, 79	8. U.S. Military Academy, 92
(tie) Michigan, 79	(tie) Wake Forest, 92
10. Wake Forest, 78	(tie) U.S. Air Force Academy, 92

Male Student-Athletes

Federal Rate	*GSR*
1. Stanford, 90	1. U.S. Naval Academy, 98
2. Notre Dame, 87	2. Notre Dame, 97
3. Duke, 85	3. Northwestern, 95
4. Northwestern, 83	(tie) Boston College, 95
5. Boston College, 80	(tie) Duke, 95
6. Vanderbilt, 77	6. Stanford, 94
7. Penn State, 75	7. U.S. Air Force Academy, 92
8. SMU, 74	8. U.S. Military Academy, 91
9. Wake Forest, 72	(tie) Vanderbilt, 91
10. Rice, 71	10. Wake Forest, 89

Female Student-Athletes

Federal Rate	*GSR*
1. Notre Dame, 93	1. Notre Dame, 100
(tie) Northwestern, 93	(tie) Vanderbilt, 100
3. Duke, 92	(tie) U.S. Naval Academy, 100
4. Rice, 91	4. Northwestern, 99
(tie) Penn State, 91	(tie) Duke, 99
(tie) Stanford, 91	(tie) Rice, 99
7. Michigan, 90	7. Wake Forest, 98
8. Boston College, 89	(tie) Illinois, 98
9. Miami (Ohio), 88	(tie) Boston College, 98
10. Wake Forest, 87	10. Penn State, 97
	(tie) Bowling Green, 97

Black Student-Athletes

Federal Rate

1. Notre Dame, 84
2. Wake Forest, 82
(tie) Stanford, 82
4. Northwestern, 81
5. Vanderbilt, 77
(tie) Duke, 77
7. Penn State, 76
8. Boston College, 72
(tie) Rice, 72
10. Marshall, 69
(tie) Southern Mississippi, 69

GSR

1. U.S. Naval Academy, 98
2. Notre Dame, 96
3. Northwestern, 94
4. Wake Forest, 89
(tie) Duke, 89
6. U.S. Air Force Academy, 86
(tie) Vanderbilt, 86
8. Stanford, 85
9. Boston College, 84
10. U.S. Military Academy, 82

Football Student-Athletes

Federal Rate

1. Stanford, 89
2. Boston College, 88
3. Duke, 86
4. Notre Dame, 85
5. Vanderbilt, 81
6. Northwestern, 78
7. Nebraska, 75
(tie) Penn State, 75
9. Cincinnati, 73
10. Rice, 71

GSR

1. U.S. Naval Academy, 95
2. Notre Dame, 94
3. Stanford, 93
4. Northwestern, 92
(tie) Boston College, 92
(tie) Duke, 9
7. Vanderbilt, 91
8. U.S. Air Force Academy, 90
9. U.S. Military Academy, 87
10. Wake Forest, 83
(tie) Miami (Ohio), 83

Since the NCAA first published GSR numbers in 2005, here are the trends for Notre Dame in all 10 categories over the four years of graduation rates (includes ranking and raw graduation percentage; "SA" stands for student-athletes):

Category	2005	2006	2007	2008
All SAs Fed.	1st at 90	2nd at 89	3rd at 89	2nd at 89
GSR	2nd at 98	2nd at 98	1st at 98	1st at 98
Male SAs Fed.	1st at 87	1st at 87	3rd at 85	2nd at 87
GSR	2nd at 98	2nd at 97	2nd at 97	2nd at 97
Female SAs Fed.	1st at 96	2nd at 94	1st at 94	1st at 93
GSR	5th at 99	2nd at 99	1st at 100	1st at 100
Black SAs Fed.	6th at 78	6th at 84	8th at 75	1st at 84
GSR	6th at 93	3rd at 95	4th at 91	2nd at 96
Football SAs Fed.	4th at 85	6th at 84	6th at 79	4th at 85
GSR	2nd at 96	3rd at 95	3rd at 93	2nd at 94

Over the four years worth of numbers of both the federal rates and the GSR, Notre Dame had 40 possible rankings in the five categories (among the FBS institutions) and 11 times ranked first, 14 times ranked second, and five times ranked third.

In addition to graduation rates, the Irish boast four former football players who have been selected to the GTE Academic All-America Hall of Fame—Joe Theismann (1990), Dave Casper (1993), Bob Thomas (1996), and Bob Burger (2006).

Thirty Notre Dame football players have been first-team Academic All-Americans—including three-time honoree Joe Heap (1952–54) and two-time selections Tom Gatewood (1970–71), Greg Marx (1971–72), Joe Restic (1977–78), and Tim Ruddy (1992–93), along with most recent honoree John Carlson (2006).

Irish football players have won NCAA Post-Graduate Scholarships on 16 occasions (Carlson was the most recent in 2007). Fifteen times Irish players have won National Football Foundation scholarships (Carlson won one of those, too).

41 The NBC Contract

Football Exposure Produces Scholarship Funding

There may have been no bigger change in the college football broadcasting landscape than what came about on a Monday in February 1990 when the University of Notre Dame and NBC Sports jointly announced that the university had sold the rights to televise home football games for the next five years (1991–95) to the network.

The NCAA had long held the television rights, meaning even the most successful programs in the country appeared once or twice per season (one regional, one national). The last NCAA contract allowed for five appearances over a two-year period—and the rest of a team's games went un-televised.

The Universities of Georgia and Oklahoma ended that relationship when they filed suit against the NCAA and won on a 1984 Supreme Court ruling. The College Football Association, under the direction of former Big Eight Conference commissioner Chuck Neinas, inherited the national rights for a handful of years for most major conferences (except the Big Ten and the Pacific-10 Conferences). However, the CFA's plan to look at a schedule of more regional games prompted Notre Dame to have a conversation with NBC, with whom it already had a relationship in men's basketball.

The Notre Dame–NBC agreement shocked the college football world, mainly because it came as a surprise to most and qualified as the first national television deal involving a single institution.

Arguably, the deal increased the number of national appearances for college football at large, considering NBC had not been in the college football business other than for events such as the Rose, Cotton, and Orange Bowls.

In fact, from 1991 through the 2008 season, 36 different Irish opponents made one or more national appearances on NBC by coming to Notre Dame Stadium to play.

The Irish home games received solid visibility to begin the series, in part because NBC assigned Dick Enberg and the late Bill Walsh as its initial broadcast team. NBC alternated announcers within individual seasons for a number of years before settling on play-by-play veteran Tom Hammond and former USC quarterback Pat Haden as its team in recent seasons.

The top-rated Notre Dame game on NBC has been the 1993 Notre Dame–Florida State contest with a 16.0 rating (39 share). Second on the list is the 1994 Notre Dame–Michigan game (8.0 rating, 22 share).

Notre Dame's record in home games on NBC is 77–33–1 (.698). The only season Notre Dame has finished unbeaten at home on NBC came in 1998, when the Irish went 6–0 in Notre Dame Stadium on their way to a 9–3 overall mark (after a Gator Bowl loss to Georgia Tech).

Recent technology innovations prompted NBC in 2007 to add a web-only pre- and post-game show (both a half-hour long), anchored by Chicago sportscaster Paula Farris (she's on the WMAQ-TV staff) and MSNBC.com sportswriter John Walters.

The network offered for the first time in 2007 its streamlined online "shortcut" version of the game that features plays only and lasts about 20 minutes. Then, in 2008, NBC began pushing the game to mobile carriers AT&T and Verizon, as well as offering both highlights and a full-game replay on the popular hulu.com site.

Any way you look at it, the Notre Dame–NBC relationship is a long way from the old days of a couple of television appearances per season under the NCAA rules. As *Sports Illustrated*'s Dan Jenkins put it, "The long-suffering multitudes have been conditioned to watching Brigham Young vs. Wyoming when the world knows that at that very moment Notre Dame is playing USC for the whole store."

42 Tour New Notre Dame Stadium

Expansion Boosts Capacity

Notre Dame Stadium, maybe the most renowned college football facility in the nation, now qualifies as one of the most up to date as well, thanks to a major addition and renovations that boosted its capacity to more than 80,000 beginning with the 1997 campaign.

The 1996 season proved to be the final one in which the customary 59,075 fans gathered for Irish home games. Nearly two years worth of additions and improvements to the yellow-bricked arena were part of a $50 million expansion project that added more than 21,000 seats beginning with the 1997 season.

The current capacity of Notre Dame Stadium is 80,795, a figure that was modified in 2001 from 80,232. In 1997, the figure was 80,225—which was based on computerized seating projections made prior to the completion of the construction of the new seating area.

Notre Dame's football team completed its 1995 home schedule November 4 against Navy—and by the following Monday, groundbreaking ceremonies had been held and work had begun on the 21-month construction project that was completed August 1, 1997.

Elements of the construction included:

- All-field seating and the first three rows in the permanent stands were eliminated to improve sight lines.
- A new natural grass field and a new drainage system were put in place.
- Two new scoreboards were erected on the north and south ends of the Stadium.

- The Jim and Marilyn Fitzgerald Family Sports and Communications Center, a new three-tiered press box with views of both the field and the campus, was constructed on the west side—with seating for 330 media in the main portion of the press box, three television broadcast booths, five radio broadcast booths, and an overall increase in square footage almost four times the original space.

- New landscaping created a park-like setting on the periphery of the Stadium.

- The locker rooms for both Notre Dame and the visiting team more than doubled in size—with the Irish locker area also serving as a permanent area used by Irish players all year long for both games and practices (until the Gug opened in 2005). In addition, a new expanded training room was constructed adjacent to the locker room.

- Lights were installed in each corner of the Stadium bowl and on top of the press box in time for use in the final month of the 1996 season.

- Material for the project included 240,000 concrete blocks, 700,000 new bricks, 500 cubic yards of mortar, 25,000 cubic yards of cast-in-place concrete, five miles of new handrails and guardrails, and 8½ miles of redwood seating.

- More than 3,500 sheets of drawings were used to build the project.

- Eleven new openings, for a total of 31, were cut into the old Stadium brick exterior to allow fans to connect the old and new lower concourse areas.

- The lettering at the north and south canopy as well as the interlocking ND logo at the top of the press box west face are gold laminate.

- Within the design of the entry gates, fans may notice the diagonal stripes of the end zone, hash marks, and a football.

- All existing urinals were refinished as part of the renovation, and there are approximately 2½ times more new women's toilets.
- Each of the approximately 44,000 old seating brackets was sandblasted and recoated with an epoxy primer.
- Glazed brick was salvaged and reused in the expanded varsity locker area.
- Notre Dame players continue to enter the field down a set of stairs past the "Play Like A Champion Today" sign, but stairs to the visiting locker room were eliminated, with the top of the processional tunnel ramp now serving as the visiting team entrance.

Casteel Construction Corp. of South Bend was the general contractor for the project. Ellerbe Becket Inc. of Kansas City, Missouri, was the architect.

The expanded Notre Dame Stadium was dedicated on the weekend of Notre Dame's 1997 season-opening game against Georgia Tech, with events including a three-day open house, a first-ever pep rally in the Stadium the evening prior to the first game (more than 35,000 fans attended), plus a Saturday morning rededication breakfast followed by a ceremonial ribbon-cutting. Every former Notre Dame football player was offered the opportunity to purchase tickets for the Georgia Tech game, and prior to the game the '97 Irish team ran through a tunnel of those former players in attendance (those practices continue for the first home game every season).

Other elements of the weekend included a specially designed rededication logo, a commemorative video, and coffee-table book detailing the construction project and an official flip coin for the game against Georgia Tech. The official game program included a 24-page reproduction of the 1930 dedication game program and a 16-page color insert highlighting the expansion.

The Board of Trustees of the University of Notre Dame approved the plan to expand the facility on May 6, 1994. The action of the Trustees culminated a long and comprehensive review within the university of the feasibility and desirability of stadium expansion.

The project was financed primarily by the November 1994 issuance of $53 million in tax-exempt, fixed-rate bonds. The bonds were sold in 26 states and the District of Columbia, with more than 20 percent sold to retail buyers and almost 80 percent to institutional buyers.

The incremental revenues from the expansion will exceed the debt service on the bonds by $47 million over the next 30 years, allowing the project not only to pay for itself, but also to generate $47 million for academic and student life needs.

Stadium expansion was the subject of one of 43 recommendations submitted to the Trustees in May 1993 by Notre Dame's president, Rev. Edward A. Malloy, C.S.C., in his final report of the Colloquy for the Year 2000. The Colloquy was a University-wide self-study carried out by committees composed of faculty, students, and staff.

Father Malloy's report specified the conditions addressed by the approved expansion plan with regard to financing and use of stadium revenues, as well as matters of aesthetics, logistics, community relations, and communications. The plan approved by the Board of Trustees addressed each of those issues.

Impetus for the Stadium addition came in September 1991 when the national board of directors of the Notre Dame Alumni Association adopted a resolution encouraging the university to study the feasibility of expanding the stadium.

Notre Dame Stadium, at 59,075, was previously ranked 44th in seating capacity among the 107 Division I-A football facilities. With capacity increased to 80,795, it now ranks 19th—with Notre

Dame, for example, ranking eighth nationally in attendance in 1997, 11th in '98, 10th in '99, 13th in 2000, 14th in 2001, then 17th in 2007. Notre Dame's average per-game increase of 21,150 fans in '97 ranked second nationally and helped contribute to record attendance figures of 36.9 million in '97 for all of college football, including 27.5 million for Division I-A games.

Ticket Breakdown

Students	10,795
Faculty/Staff	8,000
Opponents	5,000
Season Tickets	20,000
University Allotments	7,000
Contributing Alumni	30,000+
Total	80,795

Includes University Trustees, advisory council members, alumni board, alumni clubs, major benefactors, and others.

43 The 1924 Championship Season

Ride of the Four Horsemen

The 1924 Notre Dame football team will always be best known for *New York Herald-Tribune* sportswriter Grantland Rice's account of the Notre Dame vs. Army game played October 18 at the Polo Grounds in New York:

"Outlined against a blue-gray October sky, the Four Horsemen rode again. In dramatic lore they are known as famine, pestilence, destruction, and death. These are only aliases. Their real names are Stuhldreher, Miller, Crowley, and Layden. They formed the crest of the South Bend cyclone before which another fighting Army team was swept over the precipice at the Polo Grounds this afternoon as 55,000 spectators peered down on the bewildering panorama spread out on the green plain below."

Quarterback Harry Stuhldreher, fullback Elmer Layden, and halfbacks Jim Crowley and Don Miller were the cornerstone of a team considered one of the best in college football history.

The Fighting Irish won the Army game 13–7, as the Four Horsemen played magnificently.

Miller rushed for 148 yards, Crowley for 102, and Layden for 60, while Stuhldreher orchestrated the offense masterfully from the quarterback position. It was the third victory of the season for the Irish, it came against a foe considered the toughest on the schedule, and it spurred the Irish on to a perfect 10–0 season and the school's first recognized national championship.

Rice's account led to near-mythic status for the Irish backfield, but the Seven Mules, who did the blocking, and the Shock Troops, who were perhaps the best second string in the game, played indispensable roles, too. Each week in 1924, seventh-year Notre Dame coach Knute Rockne started his second stringers, his Shock Troops.

When Rockne felt his Shock Troops had done their job, he brought in the Four Horsemen and the Seven Mules, a group so good "that the Holy Ghost couldn't have broken into that lineup," said Harry O'Boyle, a kicker and reserve halfback on the Shock Troops. Center Adam Walsh was the heart of the Seven Mules, a group that also included ends Ed Hunsinger and Chuck Collins, tackles Rip Miller and Joe Bach, and guards Noble Kizer and John Wiebel. Walsh characterized the win over Army with a late interception—which he made with two broken hands.

The combination of the Shock Troops, the Seven Mules, and the Four Horsemen worked 10 times in 10 tries in 1924 against a

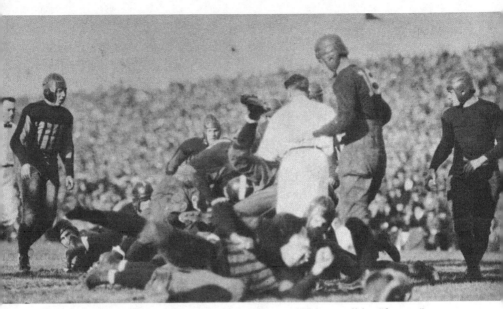

A perfect 10–0 season by the team that Rockne would later call his "favorite" brought the first national championship home to South Bend.

national schedule that took the Irish to New York, Princeton, New Jersey, Madison, Wisconsin, Soldier Field in Chicago, and Pittsburgh during the regular season while giving them only four home games. In addition, at the end of the season, Rockne was able to convince the university administration to permit the football team to travel to California to play Stanford in the Rose Bowl, where the Irish clinched the Helms Athletic Foundation's national championship with a 27–10 victory.

In the Rose Bowl—Notre Dame's only bowl appearance until the team began making regular bowl trips with the 1970 Cotton Bowl—the Irish were faced with stopping an undefeated, once-tied Stanford team that included legendary coach Pop Warner and quarterback Ernie Nevers. Rockne was concerned his players might not be ready physically for the heat of the West Coast, so he arranged for a slow, cross-country train trip that included stops in Louisiana,

Texas, and Arizona so players would have time to adjust to warmer, more demanding weather.

It worked, as Elmer Layden scored Notre Dame's first touchdown on a three-yard run and returned interceptions of Nevers' passes 78 and 70 yards for two more touchdowns. The Irish took advantage of eight Stanford turnovers and made a critical goal-line stand in the fourth quarter to come up with the 17-point win.

"That would always be my favorite team," Rockne once said. "I think I sensed that the backfield was a product of destiny. At times they caused me a certain amount of pain and exasperation, but mainly they brought me great joy."

44 The 1943 Championship Season

Start of the Leahy Dynasty in South Bend

At the beginning of the 1943 season, many experts called Notre Dame's schedule the most difficult in school history. The Irish faced seven teams that year that were ranked among the nation's top 13 teams in that season's final Associated Press Poll.

Frank Leahy's squad only had two returning starters from the 1942 squad that finished 7–2–2. To make matters worse, seven of the 10 games in '43 were on the road.

The Irish were still in the early stages of adjusting to the T-formation, which Leahy installed the season before, moving away from the traditional Notre Dame box formation. The new offense enabled the '43 team to score 340 points, 156 more than the season before. The T-formation also led to the emergence of Angelo Bertelli, who moved from tailback to quarterback to lead the Irish offense. Bertelli led the Irish to a 6–0 start as the team outscored its opponents 261–31. Included in that stretch were key victories over second-ranked Michigan and third-ranked Navy.

A record crowd of 86,408 witnessed the 35–12 Irish win in Ann Arbor. Bertelli was brilliant, completing 5-of-8 passes for two touchdowns while All-American running back Creighton Miller averaged 16 yards per play against Michigan.

Led by Bertelli and All-American tackle Jim White, both of whom finished in the top 10 in the Heisman balloting that year, the Irish rolled to a 50–0 victory over Wisconsin and a 47–0 bashing of Illinois following the win over Michigan, to extend their record to 5–0.

Those wins were followed by a colossal matchup between top-ranked Notre Dame and third-ranked Navy in Cleveland. The Irish cruised to a 33–6 win but lost their quarterback. The Marine Corps called Bertelli into service with four games left in the season. Leahy called on a sophomore to be Bertelli's replacement in the following week's game against Army, the third-ranked team in the country that week.

All Bertelli's replacement did was throw for two touchdowns, run for another, and intercept a pass to lead the Irish to a 26–0 win. A new star was born—the incomparable John Lujack.

With Lujack calling the signals, the Irish defeated two more top-10 teams in the following two weeks—Northwestern and Iowa Pre-Flight.

All that stood between Leahy's first undefeated and untied season was Great Lakes, a team the Irish had tied in their two previous meetings during the 1918 and 1942 seasons. Notre Dame scored first but trailed 12–7 late in the fourth quarter. Miller capped off an 80-yard drive with a touchdown to put the Irish ahead 14–12 with 1:05 to play.

With 33 seconds remaining, Great Lakes quarterback Steve Lach connected on a 46-yard pass to Paul Anderson, who fielded the ball at the 6-yard line and then went into the end zone for the game-winning score, ruining Notre Dame's perfect season.

After the game, Leahy told his team, "You're still champions to me, boys. You fought your hearts out every inch of the way in the greatest drive I've ever seen. Nobody is to blame for that last Great Lakes touchdown. It was just a fine play, splendidly executed."

Despite the season-ending loss, Notre Dame picked up several awards that would become commonplace for the school. The Irish were crowned national champions by the Associated Press for the first time ever, and Bertelli became the first Notre Dame player to win the Heisman Trophy. Bertelli easily outdistanced Bob O'Dell of Pennsylvania and Otto Graham of Northwestern for the Heisman.

45 The 1947 Championship Season

Maybe the Best Ever?

In any discussion of college football's greatest teams, one team that always comes to mind is the 1947 Notre Dame squad. The Irish never trailed in any game that year and compiled a 9–0 record, their first unblemished record in 17 years.

Notre Dame held its opponents to fewer than six points a game while averaging more than 32 points. Only one team—Northwestern—scored more than one touchdown against the Irish that year. But maybe the most impressive note about the squad is that it sent 42 players to professional football.

The mainstays on that team included consensus All-Americans George Connor, Bill Fischer, and John Lujack (who won the Heisman Trophy that year). The team also included future

Heisman winner Leon Hart and the man who later succeeded Leahy as head coach of the Irish, Terry Brennan.

The Irish began the season with six turnovers against Pittsburgh, but Lujack scored three times to lead Notre Dame to an easy 40–6 win. Leahy's squad stumbled a little bit in the next game, too, but came out ahead of Purdue 22–7.

Notre Dame then exploded for three consecutive shutouts over Nebraska (31–0), Iowa (21–0), and Navy (27–0). The win over the Cornhuskers avenged a 17–0 loss that Knute Rockne's 1925 squad suffered to Nebraska the last time the two schools met.

Following three impressive shutouts, the Irish faced Army, a team that had become such a fierce rival in previous years that the series was discontinued for 10 years after the 1947 game. The two teams had battled to a 0–0 tie in 1946 in one of the most famous games in Notre Dame history.

Notre Dame entered the game as the top-ranked team in the country while Army was rated eighth. The Irish struck first when Brennan broke loose for a 97-yard kickoff return. Notre Dame built a 20–0 lead before Army finally scored. The Irish won 27–7 before a record crowd of 59,171 at Notre Dame Stadium.

The next week was the only close game of the year. Northwestern became the only team in 1947 to come within two touchdowns of the Irish as Notre Dame won 26–19. The Irish ended the season with a 59–6 thrashing of Tulane and an impressive 38–7 win over third-ranked USC.

When the final national polls came out, Notre Dame was No. 1 for the second straight year.

Just how good was this 1947 team? Well, consider that several of the first-string players that year (such as Brennan) didn't even try out for professional football but opted to coach instead.

The great '47 squad also included six players who were elected into the National Football Foundation College Hall of Fame— Lujack, Connor, Hart, Fischer, Sitko, and Ziggy Czarobski. And to top that off, their coach, Frank Leahy, wound up the second-winningest coach in college history behind his mentor, Knute Rockne.

The *Boston Herald* called the '47 Irish team, "the greatest Notre Dame squad of all time. Its third string could whip most varsities."

The immortal sportswriter Grantland Rice added after the final game of the season, "There no longer is any doubt as to the best team in college football, it happens to be Notre Dame. College football never before has known a team so big, so fast, and so experienced."

His words may still hold true today.

46 The Rocket Man

Raghib Ismail

ESPN's Kirk Herbstreit rates Ismail as his best-ever wide receiver.

Ismail also qualifies as the only player in college football history to twice score on kickoff returns in two different games. He did it in 1988 against Rice at Notre Dame Stadium (78 and 83 yards)—and also did it at Michigan Stadium in Ann Arbor against second-ranked Michigan in 1989 (88 and 92 yards) in an effort that landed him on the cover of *Sports Illustrated*.

Ismail finished second to BYU quarterback Ty Detmer in the 1990 Heisman Trophy voting (1,482 points for Detmer, to 1,177 for Ismail). Interestingly enough, Detmer was not present at the Downtown Athletic Club for that December 1 announcement because his team was in Hawaii for a game later that night against the Rainbow Warriors—and Detmer threw four interceptions in that contest in a 59–28 loss to Hawaii (he did complete 22-of-45 throws for 319 yards and three touchdowns).

Then, in the bowl games, Ismail made one of the most sensational plays that didn't count when he ran back a punt 91 yards for a score in the final minutes against top-rated Colorado, only to have a penalty call it back and preserve a 10–9 win for the Buffs. Meanwhile, Detmer and BYU lost 65–14 to Texas A&M in the Holiday Bowl, with Detmer suffering multiple shoulder separations and completing only 11-of-23 passes for 120 yards (with one touchdown and one interception).

In its 2008 release, *The College Football Book, Sports Illustrated* rated Ismail on its 1980s all-decade unit.

Still, Ismail at times was something of a sheepish superstar. As a rookie wide receiver on Notre Dame's 1988 national title team, he was able to effectively blend in during a season more dominated by defense, while he continued his personal adjustment from being a running back in high school to a full-time receiver in South Bend.

All that changed with his two kickoff returns in Ann Arbor and his appearance on *Sports Illustrated* (billing him as "The Rocket Man"). Ismail's anonymity was gone for good by that time, yet he honestly often felt his older teammates should be receiving more of the publicity. He carried that reticence to such great lengths that on one occasion he had Irish student managers hide him in the equipment bin with dirty uniforms so he could be rolled away from the locker room without having to speak to the media. It's ironic since the effervescent Ismail had some success in the media himself, working with the ESPN *College GameDay* operation for several seasons.

Ismail led the nation in kickoff returns in 1988 with his 36.1-yard average. He rated ninth in all-purpose running in '90 at 156.91 yards per game, as well.

He led the team in kickoff returns three straight seasons from 1988–90. He was the leading Irish receiver for the season with 27 catches for 537 yards in '89 and 32 more for 699 in '90. Like Tim Brown before him, Ismail benefited from Lou Holtz's emphasis on the flanker position with his ability to carry the football as a running back in some formations.

More than anything, Ismail brought such an excitement level to the stadium, that almost anytime he dropped back to return a kickoff or punt, the crowd rose to its collective feet in anticipation of something special.

And more often than not, he delivered.

The Wilkes-Barre, Pennsylvania, product was named national player of the year in 1990 by both *The Sporting News* and the Walter Camp Foundation. He was also an NCAA runner-up in indoor track in the 55-meter dash in 1991 (he holds the Notre Dame record at 6.07 seconds).

Ismail again made the cover of *Sports Illustrated* after signing with the Toronto Argonauts of the Canadian Football League— then after two seasons, he came to the NFL and played for the Los Angeles Raiders, Carolina Panthers, and Dallas Cowboys. He led the Cowboys in receiving yards in 2001—in what was his final pro season. He had 28 NFL touchdown receptions and once was timed at 4.16 seconds for the 40-yard dash at Notre Dame.

Ismail had two 1,000-yard receiving seasons in the NFL and was a CFL All-Star in 1991, as well as the most valuable player of the 79th Grey Cup.

In 2004, CollegeFootballNews.com listed Ismail as the 75th player on its list of the Top 100 Greatest College Football Players of All-Time.

47 The Ice Bowl

The 1979 Cotton Bowl vs. Houston

Notre Dame utilized a miracle rally beginning midway through the fourth period to shock Houston 35–34 and capture the 43rd and coldest Cotton Bowl to conclude the 1978 season. It featured a comeback that many longtime observers called the greatest in Irish football history.

Quarterback Joe Montana, who missed most of the third quarter because of below-normal body temperature, captained an Irish rescue mission that saw the gold and green put 23 points on the board in the final 7:37, erasing a 34–12 Cougar lead in the process.

What happened in the last 7:37 was mind-boggling. For starters, the tide turned when freshman reserve fullback Tony Belden blocked a Jay Wyatt punt and classmate Steve Cichy picked it up in a crowd and rambled 33 yards for an Irish score. Notre Dame, electing to go for two, narrowed the deficit to 34–20 when Montana connected with tailback Vagas Ferguson in the end zone.

After his team had forced another Wyatt punt, Montana shifted into overdrive when the Irish regained possession at their own 39-yard line with 5:40 remaining on the clock.

On three consecutive plays the senior quarterback completed passes and connected with freshman tight end Dean Masztak, fullback Jerome Heavens, and flanker Pete Holohan for respective gains of 17, 30, and 11 (the last one on pass interference) yards. Two plays later Montana swept left end for two yards and a touchdown. Two points were once again a must for the Irish, who brought the score to 34–28 with a Montana-to-Haines completion.

Quarterback Joe Montana needed a dose of hot chicken soup to combat the effects of frigid conditions in the 1979 Cotton Bowl and lead the team to one of the greatest comeback victories in history.

The once-dumbfounded Notre Dame legions suddenly had reason to cheer. Their Irish were rolling, or so it seemed, until all momentum seemed to disappear with 2:05 left in the game—Montana fumbled after a 16-yard run to the Houston 20, and Cougar Tommy Ebner recovered.

The Irish defense stiffened, and with a fourth-and-1 from the Cougar 29 and 35 seconds left, Yeoman overruled a possible punt to go for the first down that would seal a win for the Southwest Conference champions. But Notre Dame held on a stop by freshman Joe Gramke, and the Irish took over with 28 ticks of the clock left just 29 yards short of paydirt.

Montana, who needed a dose of chicken soup to help erase his hypothermic condition, started the last-ditch Irish effort by running for 11 yards and then throwing to Haines for a gain of 10.

On the next play, Montana, the same Montana who had earlier thrown four interceptions, wasted little time getting rid of the ball, tossing it quickly to the right corner of the end zone and in the direction of Haines. The pass was incomplete, but Montana's quickness in releasing stopped the clock with two seconds remaining and gave the Irish one last chance.

Montana, calling for the same play twice in a row, then proceeded to hit Haines with the tying touchdown pass.

Joe Unis, a Dallas native, came on to kick the extra point. An illegal procedure penalty nullified the winning point, so Unis had to do it all over.

He did, and the miracle was history.

48 Bowl Revival Part II

The 1971 Cotton Bowl vs. No. 1 Texas

Notre Dame's defense caused nine Texas fumbles and All-American quarterback Joe Theismann personally accounted for three scores in the first 16-and-a-half minutes en route to a 24–11 Irish victory in the 1971 Cotton Bowl Classic.

The victory, Notre Dame's tenth against only one loss during the season, stopped the Longhorns' 30-game winning string and knocked top-ranked Texas out of the race for its second consecutive national championship. The decisive win was the first bowl victory in 46 years for Notre Dame, who returned to the postseason scene the year before after a 45-year absence.

Both teams displayed their offensive fireworks in the first half, as the Irish built up a 24–11 advantage that held up until the final gun. Texas cracked the scoring barrier early in the first period on Happy Feller's 23-yard field goal. On the first play of the Texas possession, quarterback Eddie Phillips rambled 63 yards downfield on an option play.

But the Notre Dame defense stiffened its resistance, and the Longhorns had to settle for only the three-pointer.

Theismann ignited the Notre Dame charge by rallying the Irish to three touchdowns on their next four possessions. The senior All-Star guided the Irish 80 yards in only 10 plays and tossed a 26-yard pass to Tom Gatewood for the touchdown. The scoring march included another Theismann pass to Gatewood (this one for 17 yards) and a Theismann scamper of 12 yards, along with runs of seven, 11, and six yards by John Cieszkowski. Scott Hempel's kick gave the Irish a 7–3 lead, and they never looked back.

Notre Dame increased its lead by seven just two-and-a-half minutes later. Tom Eaton recovered a Texas fumble on the kickoff at the Longhorn 13-yard line. Six plays later, Theismann took the ball in himself on a three-yard run. Hempel converted the PAT.

The Irish scored again on another Theismann run—this one from 15 yards—early in the second period. He helped the Irish march the 53 yards in the drive by tossing a 19-yard pass to Mike Creaney. Ed Gulyas contributed a 12-yard run.

Although the Longhorns had trouble getting their famed Wishbone attack off the ground because of a unique Notre Dame defensive alignment, Texas did manage another score in the second period. Phillips abandoned the run and went to the most rusty weapon in the Longhorn arsenal—the pass. He hit tight end Deryl Comer three times (for eight, 36, and 10 yards) in an 84-yard drive that climaxed on Jim Bertelsen's two-yard run. A Phillips pass to Danny Lester added two points.

The Irish wrapped up the scoring on a 36-yard field goal by Hempel with 24 seconds remaining on the clock before intermission.

The second half turned into a defensive struggle as Notre Dame played it conservatively, and Texas tried to figure out the Irish defensive setup that featured six men on the line of scrimmage—with three across from the Longhorn center.

Neither team mounted much of a scoring threat. However, in the third period, the fired-up Notre Dame defense took the steam out of a promising Longhorn drive. Irish linebacker Jim Musuraca met Bertelsen head-on at the Notre Dame 35-yard line and forced another fumble, one of five recovered by the Irish, which gave the ball and the momentum to Notre Dame.

Texas, who entered the game as the nation's top-ranked rushing team with an average of 374 yards per game, managed only 216 yards against the Irish. Phillips accumulated 164 of those yards. Notre Dame's ground game netted only 146 yards paced by Cieszkowski's 52-yard effort.

Phillips, who combined for 363 yards total offense, erased Theismann's standard of 279 set the previous year. He was voted the top offense player, while Notre Dame's Clarence Ellis earned the defensive honor.

49 Ara's Final Game

The 1975 Orange Bowl vs. No. 1 Alabama

In 1975, Alabama and Notre Dame locked horns again.

Although the stakes weren't as high (only Alabama was ranked number one, undefeated, and looking for a national championship), the atmosphere was just as electric and frenzied as the 1973 Sugar Bowl that ended the previous season for the same two teams. And this game was to be Ara Parseghian's last as head coach at Notre Dame. After 11 successful seasons and two national championships, he was hanging up his coach's playbook.

The Fighting Irish, though decided underdogs with their 9–2 ledger, gave Parseghian a proper going-away present—a 13–11 victory that denied the Tide the national title for the second straight year and gave Alabama and coach Paul "Bear" Bryant its eighth consecutive non-win in bowl competition.

Notre Dame staked itself to a 13–0 lead midway through the opening half and withstood the Tide's offensive thrust until the final gun sounded. The Irish got their first touchdown in the opening period. Alabama fumbled a Tony Brantley punt, and Al Samuel recovered the ball at the Tide's 16-yard line.

Three plays later, Notre Dame faced a fourth-and-1 call at the 7-yard line. Wayne Bullock powered his way over the left side for three yards and a crucial first down. On the next play, he slithered into the end zone on a four-yard jaunt for the first Irish score. Dave Reeve added the extra point.

With 50 seconds left in the first quarter, the Notre Dame offense took control at its own 23-yard line and quarterback Tom Clements engineered another scoring drive—this one encompassing 77 yards in 17 plays and taking 7:21 off the clock. The Irish attempted only one pass in the march, a nine-yard completion to Mark McLane. The running game featured McLane and Samuel working the sweeps and Bullock collecting his yardage up the middle.

The drive almost stalled at the Alabama 28-yard line when the Irish faced a fourth-and-4 situation. But an offside call against the Tide on the Irish field-goal attempt gave Notre Dame new life. The Irish made the most of that resurrection, as McLane took a pitchout and ran 12 yards. Two plays later he twisted loose from the Alabama defense and went nine yards for the score. Reeve's kick was off the mark and Notre Dame had to settle for a 13–0 lead.

The Irish fumbled on their next possession and gave the Tide the football on the Notre Dame 40-yard line. Alabama's game plan was to go to the air, and quarterback Richard Todd hit Ozzie Newsome for 11 yards and Jerry Brown for 12 yards to help the Tide move to the Notre Dame 8-yard mark. But the Irish defense dug in, and Alabama could manage only a 21-yard field goal by Danny Ridgeway.

The Irish held off the Crimson Tide to give coach Ara Parseghian a victorious 13–11 going-away present in the 1975 Orange Bowl.

After a scoreless third quarter in which the Irish held Alabama to just three first downs, all by passing, Notre Dame took over at its own 8-yard line. The offense, dormant since the second quarter, surged to life. Samuel picked up 20 yards on a pair of sweeps to get the Irish out of the hole. But the Tide stopped a fourth-down try and immediately went to work.

Again, Alabama, which had averaged only 11 passes a game during the season, went to the air. Todd carried the Tide to the Irish 12-yard line but then delivered an interception to John Dubenetzky, who returned the ball 16 yards to the 26.

The Irish couldn't put together a sustained drive and turned the ball over to Alabama with 4:29 left. On fourth-and-5, Todd let loose a 48-yard touchdown pass to Russ Schamun. The Tide added two points on a conversion pass from Todd to George Pugh.

Alabama got the ball back with less than two minutes remaining. Needing only a field goal to avenge the 24–23 loss in the 1973 Sugar Bowl, Todd tossed to Schamun for a 16-yard gain and to Randy Billinsley for an eight-yard reception. But Reggie Barnett intercepted Todd's next throw and sealed the verdict in favor of the Irish.

50 The Standoff

The 1946 Army Game

Once again Notre Dame found itself in the middle of a classic confrontation.

Old rivals Army and Notre Dame were scheduled to meet in New York City's Yankee Stadium in 1946. Although the Cadets had won 25 straight and appeared headed for their third consecutive national championship, World War II was over, Frank Leahy was back from the navy, and many former Irish players were trading in their military uniforms for football jerseys.

The Army–Notre Dame game would be the game of the year. Yankee Stadium had been sold out since June even though tickets didn't go on sale publicly until August 1. More than $500,000 in refund checks were issued to disappointed fans. Requests for press credentials reached record levels, and many lucky ticket holders were blatantly scalping them for $200.

While Leahy was serving in the navy, Notre Dame had been whitewashed twice by the Cadets—59–0 in 1944 and 48–0 in 1945. Leahy had listened to those games overseas, and now that he was back, he was determined to change things.

His Irish methodically pounded their first five opponents into the ground, setting the stage for a battle of the "unbeatens" in Yankee Stadium. The week before the game, his squad would take periodical breaks during practice to chant, "Fifty-nine and forty-eight, this is the year we retaliate." Notre Dame students sent daily postcards to Army coach Earl "Red" Blaik. All were signed "SPATNC"—Society for the Prevention of Army's Third National Championship.

But the game of the year failed to answer any questions about supremacy in the college football world. The brutal, hard-fought struggle ended in a 0–0 tie.

"I suppose I should be elated over the tie," mused Leahy after the game. "After all, we didn't lose, but I'm not."

Blaik echoed his thoughts. "There is no jubilation in this dressing room. It was a vigorously fought, terrific defensive game. Both teams played beautifully on the defense, and that affected both teams' attacks."

Neither squad mustered much of a scoring threat all afternoon. Notre Dame drove all the way to the Army 4-yard line in the second quarter, but the Black Knights stopped the Irish on downs.

Notre Dame had moved the ball mostly by running down the right side.

When the Irish advanced the ball to the Navy 4-yard line, the Irish ran two quarterback sneaks. Following those attempts, the Irish ran two plays to the left but failed to score.

Notre Dame's defense contained Army's touchdown twins—Doc Blanchard and Glenn Davis—who were often caught behind the line of scrimmage.

But Blanchard, frustrated by an Irish line that refused to budge, made a last-ditch effort to score, and he almost succeeded. Army crossed into Notre Dame territory for the first and only time all day as Blanchard, "Mr. Inside," broke around the end, cut for the sideline, and had a clear path to the end zone. Only one man was in a position to try and stop him. As 74,000 fans leapt to their feet, John Lujack sped across the field, closed in on his prey, and dove for Blanchard's ankles. The All-American was dragged down on the Notre Dame 37-yard line.

"They said Blanchard couldn't be stopped one-on-one in the open field, yet I did it," said an exhausted Lujack after the game. "I really can't understand all the fuss. I simply pinned him against the sideline and dropped him with a routine tackle."

Army then moved the ball to the Notre Dame 12-yard line and Davis threw an option pass, which was intercepted by future Irish head coach Terry Brennan at the 8-yard line. One play later, Brennan ran the ball past the Irish 30, and Notre Dame was out of trouble.

Even the statistics couldn't pinpoint a clear-cut winner. Notre Dame had 10 first downs to Army's nine; the Cadets gained 224 yards, while Notre Dame managed 219. Each team had 52 yards passing and 40 yards punting. Army completed 4-of-16 passes; the Irish were 5-of-17.

51 The Fighting Irish

How the Nickname Came About

Exactly where and how Notre Dame's athletic nickname, the Fighting Irish, came to origination has never been perfectly explained.

One story suggests the moniker was born in 1899 with Notre Dame leading Northwestern 5–0 at halftime of a game in Evanston, Illinois. The Wildcat fans supposedly began to chant, "Kill the fighting Irish, kill the fighting Irish," as the second half opened.

Another tale has the nickname originating at halftime of the Notre Dame–Michigan game in 1909. With his team trailing, one Notre Dame player yelled to his teammates—who happened to have names like Dolan, Kelly, Glynn, Duffy, and Ryan—"What's the matter with you guys? You're all Irish and you're not fighting worth a lick."

Notre Dame came back to win the game and the press, after overhearing the remark, reported the game as a victory for the "Fighting Irish."

The most generally accepted explanation is that the press coined the nickname as a characterization of Notre Dame athletic teams, their never-say-die fighting spirit and their Irish qualities of grit, determination, and tenacity. The term likely began as an abusive expression tauntingly directed toward the athletes from the small, private, Catholic institution. Notre Dame alumnus Francis Wallace popularized it in his *New York Daily News* columns in the 1920s.

The Notre Dame *Scholastic*, in a 1929 edition, printed its own version of the story. "The term 'Fighting Irish' has been applied to Notre Dame teams for years. It first attached itself years ago when the school, comparatively unknown, sent is athletic teams away to play in another city.... At that time the title 'Fighting Irish' held no glory or prestige.

"The years passed swiftly and the little school began to take a place in the sports world.... 'Fighting Irish' took on a new meaning. The unknown of a few years past has boldly taken a place among the leaders. The unkind appellation became symbolic of the struggle for supremacy of the field.... The term, while given in irony, has become our heritage.... So truly does it represent us that we are unwilling to part with it."

Notre Dame competed under the nickname "Catholics" during the 1800s and became more widely known as the "Ramblers" during the early 1920s in the days of the Four Horsemen.

University President Rev. Matthew Walsh, C.S.C., officially adopted "Fighting Irish" as the Notre Dame nickname in 1927.

52 Take in a Notre Dame-USC Game

It's an Unparalleled Rivalry

Talk about rivalries all you like—Michigan–Ohio State, Auburn-Alabama, Stanford-California, USC-UCLA, Harvard-Yale, Texas-Oklahoma, and so on. They've all got great tradition, but all of them are also heavily based on geography as much as anything else.

The exception? Try Notre Dame and USC, two of the most tradition-rich programs in America. They've met every year since 1926 (actually the wives of Knute Rockne and USC's Howard Jones had more than a little to do with enacting this relationship), except for war years 1943–45. And seldom has there not been something noteworthy on the line.

In even years, USC flies cross-country to South Bend to meet the Irish in mid-October, generally when the leaves are turning and making the campus a gorgeous fall landscape. In odd years, Notre Dame returns the favor, generally for a Thanksgiving weekend meeting.

In 80 games (through 2008), both teams have been ranked 31 times (actually, there was no Associated Press poll until 1936, 10 games into the series). Seven times Notre Dame has come in ranked No. 1 (and won five of those games). Five times the Trojans have come in rated atop the AP poll (and lost three times).

In 1988, both teams were unbeaten when they met. Notre Dame came in first and USC second, with the Irish winning 27–10 on the way to the national title. In nine straight seasons from 1972–80, both teams came in ranked—and 10 of those 18 rankings were sixth or better.

In recent years, the series has run in streaks. USC won five straight (1978–82), then the Irish went 13 years (1983–95) without losing (one tie in 1994). USC has currently won seven straight (2002–08).

The list of game stars is gaudy on both sides, and Notre Dame–USC remains the most glamorous rivalry in all of college football.

"Rudy"

The Inspiring Story of Dan Ruettiger
Dan Ruettiger spent the first 27 years of his life preparing for 27 seconds of college football glory. He has spent the rest of his life making sure that everyone hears his story.

Daniel "Rudy" Ruettiger had a familiar dream. Like many young men of his generation, Rudy imagined himself in a gold helmet running through the tunnel at Notre Dame Stadium as a member of the Fighting Irish.

What separated Rudy from so many others was his fanatical devotion to this impossible dream. Rudy's work ethic far outstripped his talent. His high school grades were far from outstanding. As one of 14 children, Rudy's family in Joliet, Illinois, could not afford to send him to college. Rudy's dreams lay dormant for several years, and he spent two years as a turbine operator for Commonwealth Edison. During the Vietnam war, his job was interrupted by two years in the navy. When he returned to his factory job, Rudy shared his dreams with his best friend and co-worker.

"I wanted something better," he said, "but I didn't know how to get it."

Tragedy brought Rudy the answer when his friend was killed in an accident at the power plant.

"He had told me how he regretted not going after his dreams. Then, he got [sic] killed on me. That's when I realized I was going after Notre Dame and after my dream."

At age 23, Rudy moved to South Bend and enrolled at Holy Cross College under the G.I. Bill. While attending Holy Cross, Rudy would walk to Notre Dame to watch the 1973 championship team practice. When they left the field, he put himself through the same drills.

He also worked hard in the classroom. After failing his first four tests, he turned things around to finish with a solid 3.4 grade-point average. He applied to Notre Dame after his first semester, but his application was rejected. A semester later, Rudy was rejected again. In fact, it was not until he completed Holy Cross' two-year program with honors that he was accepted to Notre Dame.

After considerable effort, Ruettiger managed to convince Notre Dame coach Ara Parseghian to give him a spot on the Notre Dame

"When you achieve one dream, dream another." Daniel "Rudy" Ruettiger's dream came true when he played the final two plays of the November 8, 1975, home game against Georgia Tech—and sacked Tech quarterback Rudy Allen to end the game. His inspiring story was immortalized in the 1993 film, Rudy, *starring Sean Astin.*

team. As a member of the scout team, Ruettiger's job was to prepare the first team by being, essentially, a living tackling dummy. His chief value was that it didn't matter if he was injured.

On his very first play, the 5'6", 185-pound Ruettiger squared off against 6'4", 255-pound Steve Neece who knocked him on his rear end. They told him to get up, and he did. Rudy got up again and again as his miniscule frame was wantonly tossed about each day at practice. Indefatigable, Rudy refused to quit.

Former teammate Willie Fry recalled, "Our attitude at first was, 'Go away.' But he wouldn't go away. Basically you had to like Rudy because you couldn't get rid of him." Eventually, Ruettiger's bruised body had earned him the respect of teammates and the coaching staff. According to Parseghian, Rudy "had earned the right to be there."

But Rudy had not yet earned the right to wear the blue and gold. At the time, NCAA rules permitted only 60 players to dress for home games. Notre Dame had more than enough scholarship players meet this limit.

After his first season, Dan Devine took over for Parseghian as head coach. Rudy had finally gained Parseghian's respect, and now he had to start all over again with Devine. He began his final year—his last chance at glory—with a clean slate.

Week after week, he checked the dress list but never found the name Ruettiger. Before the final game against Georgia Tech, cheers rose from the ranks of the players as Devine announced that Rudy would dress for the final game. Rudy's dream came true on November 8, 1975, when he ran through the tunnel into a stadium of 59,075 screaming fans.

Although he had achieved his dream of running through the tunnel, Ruettiger's chances of taking the field remained bleak. With less than a minute to play, Notre Dame's offense still held the ball.

"We almost had to use him as a split receiver," said Irish assistant George Kelly. "We were afraid time was going to run out before we got back on defense."

But then the offense scored, and Ruettiger took the field to defend the kickoff return. The ball sailed through the end zone for a touchback, and Rudy looked to the sidelines for a replacement, but none came. Ruettiger stayed in the game for the final two plays as the left defensive end.

On the first play, Rudy burst through the blockers and nearly got to Georgia Tech's quarterback, ironically named Rudy Allen. On the next play, Ruettiger ended his Notre Dame football career with an exclamation mark, sacking Allen on the game's final play. After the tackle, Rudy rose up from the ground and onto the shoulders of teammates Ron Cullins and Tom Parise who carried

Ruettiger off the field and into the locker room. Rudy's dream continued. Sweat and tears streamed down his face as teammates chanted, "Rudy, Rudy."

"I've waited 27 years for this," Rudy said. "When you achieve one dream, dream another."

Rudy had accomplished his first dream, but he was not done yet. Ruettiger refused to let his inspirational story of grit, determination, and perseverance be forgotten. After graduating from Notre Dame in 1976 with a degree in sociology, Ruettiger took a job selling insurance. Afterwards, he worked for an auto dealer and a real estate company. But all the while, Rudy pursued his new dream—to turn his story into a movie. He approached this dream with the same determination that had been his trademark at Notre Dame.

Rudy was working as the manager of a condo complex in South Bend when his new dream started to take shape. He had been in negotiation with Angelo Pizzo, one of the screenwriters for the hit sports drama *Hoosiers*, and arranged to meet him for lunch in California. After flying to California and waiting at the restaurant, Rudy discovered that he had been stood up.

So Rudy left the restaurant and tracked down a local mailman who gave him directions to Pizzo's house. Ruettiger knocked on the door, Pizzo answered and Ruettiger said, "Hi, I'm Rudy."

"Oh no," Pizzo replied. "You're everything they say you are."

If Pizzo meant relentless, he was right. In 1991, Rudy and Pizzo signed a deal with Columbia Tristar Pictures to bring *Rudy* to the big screen. The film turned out to be a smash success—tugging on the heart-strings of audiences across the country. It received two thumbs up from Siskel and Ebert and garnered Rudy an invitation to the White House for a private screening with the Clinton family. The movie brought Rudy's inspirational story to the masses, making the name "Rudy" synonymous with the underdog.

On the coattails of the movie's success, Ruettiger became a one-man industry, peddling his message that dreams can come true. These days, Rudy makes his living as a motivational speaker.

"It's okay to have dreams if you stay true to them," he says. "Because dreams can come true."

The movie was the first to be filmed on campus since *Knute Rockne, All-American* in 1940. Some of the actual movie scenes were shot at halftime of a Notre Dame home game (Boston College 1992) so the capacity crowd in attendance could be used as a backdrop. Among the "extras" making brief appearances in the film are former Notre Dame senior administrators Father Ted Hesburgh and Father Ned Joyce, as well as Ruettiger himself.

The 1993 film premiered October 13 at the Morris Center for the Performing Arts in South Bend—with Sean Astin playing Rudy.

Ruettiger now lives in Las Vegas, has written four books, and is father of two children.

54 Chris Zorich

An Irish All-Star On and Off the Field

There's a familiar face these days in the Notre Dame athletics department.

Former Irish football All-American and recent College Football Hall of Fame inductee Chris Zorich returned to the university in the summer of 2008 to join the Irish athletics administration as manager of student welfare and development.

A 6'1", 266-pound nose tackle who played football for the Irish from 1988–90, the Chicago, Illinois, product won the 1990

Lombardi Award as the top lineman in the country. He was a two-time consensus All-America selection in 1989 and 1990 and a unanimous first-team All-American as a senior in 1990.

Zorich started at nose tackle in 1988 on Notre Dame's national championship team, making 70 tackles plus three-and-a-half sacks for minus-17 yards. In 1989 he was named United Press International Lineman of the Year and College Lineman of the Year by the Touchdown Club of Washington, D.C. He was also a finalist for the 1989 Lombardi Award.

As a senior in 1990, Zorich was chosen CBS Sports/Chevrolet Defensive Player of the Year and was a finalist for the Outland Trophy. His career totals included 219 tackles (21 for minus-56 yards).

Captain of the Irish football team his senior year, he also helped the Irish win a record 23 straight games in 1988–89, was MVP of the Orange Bowl in 1991 against top-rated Colorado, and was a member of the Walter Camp Foundation's College Football All-Century Team (2000).

In 2007, Zorich was inducted into the College Football Hall of Fame as one of the best defensive linemen to ever play the collegiate game. Not only was he one of the youngest players to ever be inducted, he is only the third defensive lineman from Notre Dame to call the College Football Hall of Fame home.

Drafted in the second round of the NFL Draft by the Chicago Bears in 1991, he played with the Bears through the first half of 1997, then played the last half of that season with the Washington Redskins.

While also serving as chairman of the Chris Zorich Foundation in Chicago, he graduated from law school at Notre Dame in 2002. He had previously earned his Bachelor of Arts degree in American Studies in 1991. While attending the Notre Dame Law School, he served clients at the Notre Dame Legal Aid Clinic, a non-profit organization designed to provide free legal assistance to those with minimal resources.

All-American nose tackle. College Football Hall of Fame inductee. Chicago Bear. Washington Redskin. Humanitarian. Attorney. Chris Zorich is the pride of the Fighting Irish.

Upon graduation, Zorich worked for the Chicago law firm of Schuyler Roche, P.C. for four years, working in the business enterprise and estate management practice areas. He was also the community outreach and marketing consultant for the firm.

Recognized for his fierce commitment on and off the playing field, Zorich has received a score of athletic and community service awards, including the following: selection as an alternate for the 1993 NFL Pro Bowl; the 10th Anniversary All-Madden Team; two-time NFL Man of the Year finalist; the NFL Players' Association's Byron "Whizzer" White Award for Community Service; and USA Weekend's Most Caring Athlete.

He received the Jesse Owens Foundation's Humanitarian Award from the family of the late Olympic great Jesse Owens, as well as Muhammad Ali's limited commission Humanitarian Award. He has also received honorary degrees from East West University, Northwestern Business College, St. Xavier University, and Governors State University.

In 2008, Zorich was appointed to The Knight Commission on Intercollegiate Athletics, an organization that serves as a watchdog group for the NCAA and seeks to reform various issues including recruiting, gender equity, and academic eligibility. He has also served as a board member for various non-profit organizations including the Chicago Public Library, the Big Shoulders Fund, the Joffrey Ballet, Special Children's Charities, and Urban Prep Academies. He was also a member of the Board of Trustees at Lewis University and the Illinois College of Optometry.

In 1993, The Christopher Zorich Foundation (www. chriszorich.org) was established to honor Chris' mother, who passed away his senior year at Notre Dame, just after Zorich's final collegiate appearance in the Orange Bowl. The Zora Zorich Scholarship is bestowed annually at the University of Notre Dame and Lewis University.

Other success stories of Zorich's foundation have included:

- Youth programs providing cultural, educational, and entertainment activities.
- Thanksgiving grocery home deliveries to 1,500 Chicagoans.
- Women's recognition on Mother's Day through flower and cosmetics deliveries to various women's shelters.

- Holiday gift programs providing gifts and matching sponsors with disadvantaged children and families.

These combined programs have assisted more than 150,000 individuals.

In 1998, Notre Dame commissioned the Christopher Zorich Award to recognize the contributions of student-athletes to the University community and the community at large.

A nationally acclaimed motivational speaker, Zorich for three years co-hosted "Bears Extra," a live weekly television show dedicated to the Chicago Bears. He was also an analyst for Comcast SportsNet's coverage of the Chicago Bears. For two years he hosted "PrepsPlus," the Midwest's highest-ranked high school sports television show. He has also moderated various town hall meetings on a variety of topics, including race and gender issues, the influence of sports in our society, and the influence of drugs on America's youth.

55 Alan Page

Notre Dame's Most Decorated Gridder

Alan Page remains one of the most accomplished football players in Notre Dame history based on his membership on the 1966 national championship roster and his first-team All-America honors.

Yet it's his impressive list of off-the-field accomplishments that has contributed to Page qualifying as the most highly recognized football player in Irish annals.

Page, now a Minnesota Supreme Court Justice, served as Notre Dame's 2004 commencement speaker. Previously the recipient of an honorary doctor of laws degree from Notre Dame, Page was honored at the 2004 ceremony with an honorary doctor of humane letters degree.

Page became the 37th recipient of the Theodore Roosevelt Award during the 2004 NCAA Honors Dinner. The coveted "Teddy," named for the 26th President who played a key role in founding the NCAA, is presented annually to a distinguished citizen of national reputation and outstanding accomplishment. It qualifies as the highest honor presented by the NCAA to a student-athlete.

After his All-America career at Notre Dame—which included a three-year record of 25–3–2 that was capped by winning the 1966 national title—Page became a key member of the Minnesota Vikings' famed Purple People Eaters defensive line. He appeared in nine Pro Bowls during an NFL career that spanned 15 seasons, including 12 as a member of the Vikings and four with the Chicago Bears (he played for both teams in 1978). In 1971, the four-time NFC defensive player of the year became the first defensive player in NFL history to earn the league's Most Valuable Player Award.

Page—elected to the NFL Pro Football Hall of Fame in 1988 and the National Football Foundation and College Hall of Fame in 1993—worked his way through law school as a full-time student while maintaining his career as a pro football player. He earned his juris doctorate from the University of Minnesota Law School in 1978 and worked as an associate with Lindquist & Vennum in 1981 before fulfilling responsibilities as a special assistant attorney general in Minnesota's employment law division. Page served as assistant attorney general from 1987–93 when he was elected to Minnesota's Supreme Court.

A vocal proponent of education and frequent speaker at elementary schools, Page and his wife Diane established the Page Education Foundation in 1988 to help provide educational grants for students of color to attend colleges in Minnesota. As a condition of receiving the funds, the Page Scholars serve as role models and mentors for younger children with the goal of changing the

For his outstanding contributions on and off the field, Alan Page became just the 37th recipient of the Theodore Roosevelt Award during the 2004 NCAA Honors Dinner. The "Teddy" is the highest honor presented by the NCAA to a student-athlete.

future. The foundation has awarded 3,965 grants to 1,885 students, totaling more than $2.5 million.

Page merited second-team recognition on the ABC Sports All-Time All-America team (as a defensive lineman—after first-teamers Bubba Smith, Lee Roy Selmon, Randy White, Bruce Smith, and Hugh Green).

Said longtime ABC Sports color analyst Gary Danielson (now with CBS Sports) about Page, "People used to call Alan crafty. He took such pride in his ability, and he seemed to have such a vision of where he wanted to go that he almost became unblockable. I heard stories about his ability, to time the snap count, that he would study stances and how opposing players would block him. He was the first modern lineman that changed the game and forced teams to double-team him.

"Alan was one of the first guys to change blocking schemes because you were forced to double team him. You had to account for him on every play because he was so quick coming off the ball and he was absolutely determined."

56 Watch the Helmet Painting

Those are Real Flecks of Gold

For many years, Notre Dame's football student managers would put masking tape over the faceguards and then spray-paint multiple coats of gold paint—with real flecks of gold—onto the Irish players' helmets.

That practice continued (beginning back in the 1960s) on Thursday nights before road games and on Friday nights before home games. In fact, the painting received feature billing in the movie *Rudy*. The helmet-painting took place in the bowels of the Notre Dame Stadium concourses—and the practice actually became something of a tourist attraction, given the number of fans who came to watch. By the time the Stadium was enlarged in 1997, the painting sessions were held just inside the gate at the north end zone, making it easy for fans to view. All that took place when players essentially went through a season using the same helmet every day for both practices and games.

By 2005, everything changed. The painting process was switched to early in the week, mostly to ensure better drying prior to game days. Current Irish equipment boss Henry Scroope remembers a trip to Nebraska in 2001 when the final facemask was finished only an hour before the team jumped on buses to the airport. The time change eliminated the spectator aspect of the process.

And the key to the timing change could come about because in 2005 all incoming Notre Dame players began breaking in two

One of the finest traditions in college football is the painting of the Notre Dame football helmets before each game.

different helmets during fall camp—one for use in practices and the second for use in games. By that time, Scroope had learned through a little research that most schools were using two sets of helmets—and that helped keep the game-day versions in nearer-mint condition.

The helmets are modeled after the gold dome on the top of the University of Notre Dame's main administration building. The gold dust, mixed with lacquer and lacquer thinner, comes from the South Bend–based O'Brien Paint Corporation.

In the 2005 book *Fifty Years of College Football*, the tradition of painting the helmets each week with gold dust rated as one of the top half-dozen traditions in college football.

57 "Fair-Catch" Corby, Golden Dome, Touchdown Jesus, "We're No. 1" Moses

Campus Landmarks Earn Athletic Acclaim

It's hard to miss the religious connotations at the University of Notre Dame, arguably the most famed Catholic institution of higher learning in the world.

So it should be no surprise to find statues and mosaics around the campus of Jesus Christ, Moses, and the priest who founded the university.

It also should come as no surprise on a campus long obsessed with its football that Notre Dame students would find ways to connect those religious figures with the game they cherish most:

"Fair-Catch" Corby—A campus statue placed in front of Corby Hall in 1911 depicts Chaplain William J. Corby, C.S.C., with his right arm raised in the act of giving absolution to the Irish Brigade before they went into action on the three-day Battle of Gettysburg (July 2, 1863). A duplicate statue that honors his long service to the Union cause was dedicated on the battlefield in 1910. Corby was Notre Dame's president from 1866–72 and again from 1887–91. His campus statue is known to the football faithful as "Fair-Catch Corby."

Golden Dome—One of the most famous landmarks from any college campus—and considered by many to be the nation's most-recognized Catholic landmark—Notre Dame's golden-domed administration building is topped by a 16-foot, 4,400-pound statue of Mary the Blessed Mother (the namesake of the University of Notre Dame). The statue and the dome are covered with extra-thin sheets of 23-karat gold leaf that sparkle in the midday sun and make the Dome a beacon to be seen from vantage points throughout the campus.

Library Mural ("Touchdown Jesus")—The 132-foot-high stone mosaic on the south side of the Hesburgh Library was patterned after Millard Sheet's painting, *The Word of Life*, with Christ as teacher surrounded by his apostles and an assembly of saints and scholars who have contributed to knowledge through the ages. A gift of Mr. and Mrs. Howard Phalin, the mural contains 80 different types of stone material from 16 countries, plus 171 finishes during the fabrication stage and a total of 5,714 individual pieces. The mural of Christ with upraised hands—which is visible from inside parts of Notre Dame Stadium—is often referred to as "Touchdown Jesus."

"We're No. 1" Moses—Crafted by Josef Turkalj—a protégé of Notre Dame's famed artist-in-residence Ivan Mestrovic—this bronze statue is located on the west side of Hesburgh Library. It depicts Moses in flowing robes at the foot of Mt. Sinai as he chastises the Israelites who have fallen into idolatry in his absence. His right hand is extended heavenward as he declares there is but one God (creating the reference to "We're No. 1"), while his left hand grasps the stone tablets upon which God has inscribed the Ten Commandments, with the right knee bent over as his foot crushes the head of the golden calf idol.

58 Slap the "Play Like A Champion Today" Sign

On the Way in to Notre Dame Stadium

The name Laurie Wenger may not mean much to you, even if you're a die-hard Notre Dame football fan.

And though her name may not rank up there with those of Knute Rockne, George Gipp, and the Four Horsemen in Irish lore,

A visible commitment to excellence, this sign reminds every player of the great responsibility that comes with wearing a Notre Dame uniform.

she is nonetheless responsible for the creation of one of the most familiar graphic images connected with the Notre Dame football program.

Wenger, who for years has worked as a sign-painter at Notre Dame's Joyce Center, received a request from new Irish coach Lou Holtz for a little assistance. Holtz wanted the phrase "Play Like A Champion Today" painted in blue and gold onto a sign that Holtz planned to place at the bottom of the Notre Dame Stadium stairwell that led to the field.

Little did anyone realize what a hit that sign would become.

It's just a simple wooden sign, with blue lettering painted on a gold background and mounted on a cream-colored brick wall at the foot of that stairwell. Yet the "Play Like A Champion Today" sign, found outside Notre Dame's locker room, has become so much more.

The slogan "Play Like A Champion Today" is now so synonymous with the University that one can be excused for believing that Father Edward Sorin, the school's founder, received it as a divine revelation in 1842.

While the exact origin of the slogan is not known, the sign that currently hangs in Notre Dame Stadium came courtesy of Holtz.

"I read a lot of books about the history of Notre Dame and its football program," Holtz says. "I forget which book I was looking at—but it had an old picture in it that showed the slogan 'Play Like A Champion Today'. I said, 'That is really appropriate; it used to be at Notre Dame and we needed to use it again.' So I had that sign made up."

Soon, the tradition of hitting the sign before every game developed. Holtz even used a copy of the sign when traveling to road contests to help motivate the team. The players took no time in embracing Holtz's idea.

"[The players] were encouraged by it; I told them the history of it; that this had been here years ago. I didn't know who took it down, I don't know why it wasn't here when I came here, but this is part of Notre Dame tradition and this is what we're going to do," Holtz said.

To Holtz—the man who resurrected what has become even a worldwide phenomenon—the hitting of the sign comes with a solemn commitment.

"Regardless of the won-lost record, regardless of the problems you have, when you walk out on that field you have an obligation to your teammates and the fans to play to the best of your ability—to play like a champion and to think like a champion," Holtz said.

"But I also asked my players that every time they hit that sign, to think about all the sacrifices your family has made; your teammates made in high school; the sacrifices your teachers have made;

and you also think of the thousands of people who would love to be in your position. Just think about how fortunate we are.

"All of these thoughts should go through your mind when you hit that sign—'Play Like A Champion Today.'"

The sign gained greater fame when NBC began televising Irish home games in 1991—and the network producers put a camera at the top of the tunnel showing the Notre Dame players as they went down the stairs and hit the sign.

Wenger says the first person to request a copy of the sign turned out to be Dan "Rudy" Ruettiger, who gained his own moment of fame when the movie *Rudy* came out.

Since the sign did not contain any of the University's protected marks or names, Wenger eventually trademarked the phrase and signed a licensing agreement with the university. She, her husband, and her father now have their own side business producing all kinds of "Play Like A Champion" products, from shirts and hats to magnets, key chains, towels—and all sorts of sizes of the sign itself.

59 The 1988–89 Win Streak

23 Skidoo

Notre Dame's all-time record 23-game winning streak from the 1988 and '89 seasons combined barely makes a splash nationally. The *Official 2008 NCAA Division I Football Records Book* lists 26 such streaks of 25 or more wins in history, so the Irish didn't even make that chart.

Nonetheless, those 23 Notre Dame victories came against an amazingly impressive list of opponents. The 23 Irish victims combined for a 145–115–8 record (73–61–4 in '88 and 72–54–4 in '89).

Of the 12 wins in 1988, five came against bowl teams: Michigan finished 9–2–1 and defeated USC in the Rose Bowl; Michigan State 6–5–1 and lost to Georgia in the Gator Bowl; Miami 11–1 and defeated Nebraska in the Orange Bowl; USC 10–2 and lost to Michigan in the Rose Bowl; and West Virginia 11–1 and lost to the Irish in the Fiesta Bowl. After Notre Dame in the final Associated Press poll came Irish opponents Miami (second), Michigan (fourth), West Virginia (fifth), and USC (seventh).

A year later in 1989, seven wins came against bowl teams: Virginia finished 10–3 and lost the Citrus Bowl to Illinois; Michigan 10–2 and lost the Rose Bowl to USC; Michigan State 8–4 and defeated Hawaii in the Aloha Bowl; Air Force 8–4–1 and lost to Ole Miss in the Liberty Bowl; USC 9–2–1 and beat Michigan in the Rose Bowl; Pittsburgh 8–3–1 and defeated Texas A&M in the Sun Bowl; and Penn State 8–3–1 and a Holiday Bowl winner over BYU. In the final AP poll, Michigan was seventh, USC eighth, Penn State 15th, Michigan State 16th, Pittsburgh 17th, and Virginia 18th.

During the streak, Notre Dame spent 19 straight weeks atop the AP poll, then the longest and now the third-longest such streak in history (longer streaks were 33 by USC in 2003–05 and 20 by Miami in 2001–02.

During the 23-game streak, Notre Dame defeated seven top-10 teams (based on ranking at the time of the games) and nine top-20 teams (11 of the 23 wins came on the road). At the time the streak ended in '89, the Irish had recorded six wins that season versus top-20 opponents and no one in the country had recorded five (and that didn't count Virginia which wasn't ranked when the Cavs played Notre Dame but was ranked with its 10–3 final mark).

Here are the combined Notre Dame statistical advantages during the streak: 34.3–13.6 in points per game, 404.0–287.4 in total yards per game, 277.8–109.4 in rushing yards per game, and 72–47 in forced turnovers.

60 The Sculptures

Leahy, Parseghian, Holtz, Moose, and Rockne

What do Frank Leahy, Ara Parseghian, Lou Holtz, Moose Krause, and Knute Rockne have in common? In addition to qualifying as iconic Notre Dame athletics figures, they are also subjects of sculptures by Jerry McKenna.

After Krause died in 1992, McKenna sculpted a version of the former Notre Dame basketball great and long-time athletics director sitting on a bench in front of the Joyce Center, with his legs crossed, wearing his signature cowboy hat and smoking a cigar.

McKenna saw his Leahy sculpture dedicated in September 1997.

The Rockne sculpture was commissioned by the College Football Hall of Fame and stands just southwest of that facility. It was dedicated in 2006—after a duplicate was placed in Voss, Norway, on the 75th anniversary of his death.

Back on the Notre Dame campus, Parseghian's former players raised funds to erect a sculpture of the Irish Hall of Fame coach just inside Gate D of Notre Dame Stadium. The work shows Parseghian raised on the shoulders of three of his players, one of them former walk-on Peter Schiavarelli who spearheaded the fundraising efforts for McKenna's work that was dedicated in September 2007.

A year later came the Holtz sculpture showing the 2008 Hall of Fame inductee calling a play from the sideline, with two of his players at his side (the players were modeled after Tim Brown and Skip Holtz).

McKenna also created a half-size sculpture of the Four Horsemen that was dedicated in September 2008 and sits in the lobby of the Guglielmino Athletics Complex, home to the Irish football offices.

61 Back in the Bowl Business

The 1970 Cotton Bowl vs. No. 1 Texas

After a 45-year absence, Notre Dame reappeared on the bowl scene.

The Irish, who headed into the battle with a respectable 8–1–1 record, drew the unenviable assignment of challenging the nation's number-one team—the unbeaten Longhorns of Texas.

With visions of the Four Horsemen (they were part of the last Notre Dame team to play in a bowl game) dancing in their heads, the Irish almost pulled off the upset. Only a 76-yard drive late in the final period, capped by Billy Dale's one-yard scoring plunge, gave the Longhorns a hard fought 21–17 victory and ensured their claim to the national title.

Although Texas won the annual Cotton Bowl Classic on this sun-drenched but chilly New Year's Day before a packed house of 73,000, Notre Dame, coached by Ara Parseghian, matched the powerful Longhorns yard for yard until the final gun.

The Irish opened the scoring in the first quarter as Scott Hempel converted a 26-yard field goal. After the opening kickoff, junior quarterback Joe Theismann guided the Irish 82 yards downfield, and ate up six minutes on the clock to set the stage for Hempel's kick.

Notre Dame scored again early in the second period as Theismann shocked the Longhorns by tossing a 54-yard touchdown bomb to Tom Gatewood on the first play from scrimmage after a Texas punt. Hempel's kick made it 10–0 for Notre Dame.

The Longhorns first lit the scoreboard in the second quarter as they drove 74 yards in nine plays. Behind the running of Ted Koy and Jim Bertelsen and the passing of James Street, the Longhorns moved into Notre Dame territory and ended the scoring march on Bertelsen's one-yard dash into the end zone. Happy Feller converted the PAT, and the Longhorns trailed 10–7.

Neither team crossed the goal line again until the final period.

Texas jumped out in front of the Irish in the fourth quarter on a bruising 77-yard drive. Steve Worster, the game's leading rusher with 155 yards, barreled his way through the Irish defense for long gains of eight, nine, and seven yards, while Bertelsen, who finished the afternoon with 81 yards, added carries of five and six yards to the Longhorn effort. Koy took the ball in from the 3-yard line, and Feller's kick gave Texas a 14–10 lead.

Notre Dame fought right back. With Theismann at the controls, Notre Dame went 80 yards in eight plays to go ahead 17–14. The feisty Theismann put together scampers of 14 and 11 yards and tossed an 11-yard pass to Dennis Allen. The Irish finally scored on a 24-yard touchdown pass from Theismann to Jim Yoder.

With seven minutes still left in the battle, coach Darrell Royal and his Longhorns weren't about to watch their national championship dreams be snuffed out. Texas made the most of its final surge. Twice the Longhorns needed conversions on fourth down to maintain possession, and the final one dashed Notre Dame's hopes.

Street, on fourth-and-2 from the Irish 10-yard line, threw low and wide to end Cotton Speyrer, but the lanky redhead snared it at the 2-yard line. The Irish defense then halted a pair of Longhorn rushing plays, but on the third try, Dale found the end zone and the Longhorns had their national championship with only 1:08 left on the clock.

Notre Dame tried another comeback attempt with the seconds ticking away. Theismann brought the Irish all the way to the Texas 39, but with 28 seconds left, Tom Campbell intercepted Theismann's final pass.

Worster earned the game's offensive player award, while Notre Dame's captain Bob Olson won the most valuable defensive player honor.

Theismann's efforts established Cotton Bowl records in two categories. His 231 yards passing broke Roger Staubach's previous mark of 228 (1964), and his 279 yards total offense surpassed Duke Carlisle's 267 standard, also set in 1964.

Dan Jenkins, who covered college football for years for *Sports Illustrated*, and Blackie Sherrod, longtime *Dallas Times-Herald* and *Dallas Morning News* columnist, called it the best bowl game in history.

62 The Leprechaun

Clenched Fists Ready for Battle

The original version of the stylized leprechaun that you see today was drawn by Elkhart, Indiana, native Ted W. Drake.

Drake is probably best remembered for that creation of the Notre Dame leprechaun for which he was paid $50 (he drew the original when he was four years old).

The leprechaun was first used on the 1964 football pocket schedule and later on football game program covers. It was featured on the cover of *TIME* on November 20, 1964—superimposed over a portrait of Irish coach Ara Parseghian.

In 1966, Drake designed the logo for the NBA Chicago Bulls basketball team.

In the early 1950s, Drake was the main graphic artist for the *Kukla, Fran and Ollie* television puppet show, creating its opening titles along with album covers, newsletters, advertisements, and even Christmas cards.

Drake's own take on the Four Horsemen has been displayed in recent years in the lobby of the Notre Dame Stadium media entrance.

63 Wayne Edmonds

Blazing a Trail at Notre Dame

As Notre Dame opened its 2008 football season, the Irish athletics department kicked off a year-long program titled "Celebrating Over 60 Years of Success by Black Student-Athletes at Notre Dame" to recognize the historical contributions of African American student-athletes at the university.

Presenting the flag prior to the Notre Dame–San Diego State season opener was Wayne Edmonds, a 1956 Notre Dame graduate and the first black football player to win a monogram while competing for the Irish. He was joined by Paul Thompson, son of Frazier Thompson, a 1947 Notre Dame graduate and former Irish track standout who was the first black graduate of the university and the first black monogram-winner in any sport at Notre Dame.

Edmonds played defensive end, tackle, and guard for the Irish in 1953, 1954, and 1955. He started at left tackle as a senior in '55 and won monograms each of those three seasons. In '53, he helped Notre Dame to a 9–0–1 mark and No. 2 final national ranking.

Listed at 6'0" and 210 pounds and originally from Canonsburg, Pennsylvania, Edmonds was selected in the ninth round of the 1956 NFL Draft by the Pittsburgh Steelers but instead

Wayne Edmonds was the first black football player to win a monogram with the Irish. He played defensive end, tackle, and guard in 1953, 1954, and 1955, and he won monograms in each of those seasons.

went to graduate school at the University of Pittsburgh and later became the dean of students at the School of Social Work at Pittsburgh.

Edmonds, who now lives in Harrisburg, Pennsylvania, majored in sociology and graduated from the College of Arts and Letters.

The return of Edmonds for the home football opener was the first of a series of events planned for 2008–09, culminating in a weekend celebration that coincided with the April 18, 2009, Blue-Gold spring football game at Notre Dame. The more than 400 African American Notre Dame monogram winners were all invited back for the events that weekend.

A commemorative logo was created to recognize the celebration, a commemorative video is in production, signage was visible around Notre Dame athletics facilities—and various interviews and feature stories appeared throughout the year in Notre Dame athletics publications and on www.und.com.

As the University highlighted the successes of black athletes at Notre Dame, remember the name Wayne Edmonds—he blazed the trails for all those who came after him.

64 The Green Jersey Tradition

There's a Place Between the Blue and Gold

Although Notre Dame's official colors for athletics have long been listed as gold and blue, the color of the Irish home football jersey has switched back and forth between blue and green for more than 50 years.

The origin of school colors can be traced back to the founding of the university. At the time of its establishment in 1842, Notre Dame's original school colors were yellow and blue; yellow symbolized the light and blue the truth. However, sometime after the Dome and Statue of Mary atop the Main Building were gilded, gold and blue became the official colors of the University.

While dark blue jerseys with a gleaming gold helmet and gold pants is the signature uniform for the Notre Dame football team, green has developed into an unofficial third school color and is used across Notre Dame's 26 varsity sports as an added inspirational tool.

Any discussion about the green uniforms in Notre Dame athletic history begins with the Notre Dame–USC contest on October 22, 1977. Irish coach Dan Devine, taking a friendly suggestion from Irish basketball coach Digger Phelps during an off-season conversation, ordered special green jerseys four months in advance of the Irish-Trojan contest. Notre Dame had not donned green jerseys since a 1963 Thanksgiving Day game in Yankee Stadium against Syracuse.

In what was billed as the best-kept secret in Irish football history, most of the team was unaware of the uniform switch until 20 minutes before kickoff, although Devine allowed captains Ross

Browner, Terry Eurick, and Willie Fry to try on the new jerseys on Friday afternoon before the pep rally. Even though Fry hinted about the change at the rally that evening by calling for the fans to wear green to the game and referring to his teammates as the "Green Machine," the secret remained safe until the team returned after pregame warm-ups to find green jerseys with gold numbers hanging in each player's respective locker.

Notre Dame Stadium was already operating at a fever pitch that day before the team even took the field. The student body wheeled a homemade Trojan horse onto the field to symbolize the historical fall of Troy. The Irish fans were also eager to make up for the 55–24 loss to USC in 1974, a game in which Notre Dame led 24–0 at halftime.

The Irish rolled to a 49–19 victory over USC in their green jerseys and the Green Machine was born. Notre Dame wore the jerseys for the rest of the season, sweeping through the remainder of the schedule and thumping No. 1 Texas 38–10 in the Cotton Bowl to earn the national championship.

Since that October day in 1977, the green jerseys have been used to give any Irish athletic team extra motivation for a big game, particularly during championship competition. Some Irish teams also have special green jerseys prepared if they are scheduled to play on St. Patrick's Day.

Gerry Faust outfitted his Irish teams in green jerseys twice for two victories over USC in 1983 and '85 (the team switched to green during halftime of the '85 game). Lou Holtz incorporated green twice in his tenure, spurring the team to a 1992 Sugar Bowl victory over Florida with green numbers on a white jersey, and the team also wore green in a 41–24 loss to Colorado in the 1995 Fiesta Bowl. Bob Davie's Irish teams wore green in a 35–28 loss to Georgia Tech in the 1999 Gator Bowl, while Tyrone Willingham's team wore green in a 14–7 loss to Boston College in 2002.

Head coach Charlie Weis employed the green jerseys against USC in 2005, and the Irish responded with a memorable performance that pushed the defending national champion Trojans to the brink in a 34–31 last-second loss. The Irish also defeated Army in '06 at Notre Dame Stadium while wearing green.

Green jerseys have developed into a special outfit for championship competition in Notre Dame's 26 varsity sports. The women's basketball team switches to green jerseys for its annual NCAA Tournament competition, which traditionally begins the same weekend as St. Patrick's Day.

In recent years, several varsity teams (men's basketball, women's basketball, baseball, hockey, softball, and women's lacrosse) have worn green jerseys while competing in a championship game or while playing on St. Patrick's Day.

Though the 1977 Notre Dame–USC gridiron contest marked the renewal of green jerseys, Notre Dame football teams have been wearing green in one fashion or another since Knute Rockne patrolled the sidelines. In those days, the Notre Dame varsity team usually wore blue, while the freshman squad was outfitted in green.

But on several occasions, the varsity team did wear green— simply for purposes of distinction when the Irish opponent also came out in blue. Games against Navy in the late 1920s, for example, featured green-clad Notre Dame teams to avoid confusion with the Navy's blue uniforms.

Rockne didn't mind using the color change as a psychological ploy. When Notre Dame faced Navy in Baltimore in 1927, the Irish head coach started his second-string reserves. Navy retaliated by scoring a touchdown in the first five minutes of the game. But just as the Midshipmen scored, reported George Trevor in the *New York Sun*, Rockne made his move:

"Instantaneously the Notre Dame regulars yanked off their blue outer sweaters and like a horde of green Gila monsters darted onto the field. From that moment on Notre Dame held the initiative, imposed its collective will upon the Navy."

The Irish came from behind to win that one 19–6—then did the same thing the following year in Chicago's Soldier Field, this time beating Navy 7–0.

The 1928 edition of the *Scholastic Football Review* included this description: "Mr. K.K. Rockne may, or may not, be a psychologist. But he did array his Fighting Irish in bright green jerseys for their battle with the United States Naval Academy. Mr. Rockne evidently surmised that garbing a band of native and adopted Irish in their native color is somewhat akin to showing a bull the Russian flag."

The green jerseys remained prominent throughout the Frank Leahy years—particularly so in September 1947 when Heisman Trophy–winner Johnny Lujack graced the cover of *Life* magazine clad in green.

Several of Joe Kuharich's squads wore green with UCLA-style shoulder stripes and shamrocks on the helmets. Even Hugh Devore's 1963 team—after wearing navy blue all season—switched to green in the finale against Syracuse.

Faust's return to blue came after the Irish coach suggested some research into the university archives to determine the history of Notre Dame's gold and blue colors. Those findings indicated the blue color was actually Madonna blue, a light blue shade, as opposed to the navy blue shade that had been most common in recent Notre Dame uniforms.

Notre Dame made moderate adjustments on its uniforms for the 2001 season as Adidas took over the design of the uniforms, adding a panel of gold down the sides of the white road jerseys with a single shamrock and the word "Irish" at the V of the neckline. A single green shamrock with an interlocking ND was also added to the traditional gold pants, while the football helmet remained the same.

Further adjustments occurred for the 2004 season as the uniform featured slimmer numbers on jerseys while removing the gold panel on the sides of the white road jerseys.

Before the Adidas-era uniform change in 2001, the 1984 season marked the most-recent major change as the Irish returned to the standard navy blue worn throughout the Ara Parseghian years and early portion of the Devine era. The gold Irish helmets and pants remained unchanged.

When Faust took over in 1981, Notre Dame went to royal blue jerseys with three one-inch stripes on the sleeves, two gold surrounding one white. But the stripes were eliminated on the '84 tops, which didn't feature any trim or feathering other than the white numbers on the navy blue shirts. Lou Holtz's only change beginning in '86 involved adding the interlocked Notre Dame logo to the shoulder of the jerseys and to the left front side of the pants.

 **Walk-Ons**

More Than Simply Names on the Roster
Notre Dame has a long history of walk-ons who have made impressive contributions on the football field.

One near the top of that list is Mike Oriard, who emerged as a starting center and team captain in 1969 after coming to Notre Dame from Spokane, Washington, without a scholarship. He went on to earn second team All-America honors and a prestigious NCAA postgraduate scholarship before playing for the NFL's

Kansas City Chiefs. Oriard is now a literature professor at Oregon State University and authored *The End of Autumn*, a book detailing his football experiences.

He's also author of *Brand NFL: Making and Selling America's Favorite Sport*, University of North Carolina Press (2007); *King Football: Sport & Spectacle in the Golden Age of Radio and Newsreels, Movies & Magazines, the Weekly & the Daily Press*, University of North Carolina Press (2001); *Reading Football: How the Popular Press Created an American Spectacle*, University of North Carolina Press (1993); *Sporting With the Gods: The Rhetoric of Play and Game in American Culture*, Cambridge University Press (1991); and *Dreaming of Heroes: American Sports Fiction, 1868–1980*, Nelson-Hall (1982).

The Irish have also featured a number of kickers in recent years who have risen from the walk-on ranks, including the likes of John Carney, Chuck Male, Mike Johnston, and Reggie Ho. Notre Dame's punter and place-kicker in 1987, Vince Phelan and Ted Gradel respectively, both were walk-ons who earned Academic All-America honors (as did Ho).

Other walk-on standouts were Bob Burger, a starting offensive guard on the team that played in the 1981 Sugar Bowl, and Mike Brennan, a converted lacrosse player who developed into a starting offensive tackle with the Irish in 1989 before going on to a career in the NFL.

More recently, soccer player Shane Walton shifted to the gridiron and went on to be an All-American cornerback and leader of Notre Dame's 10–3 team in 2002, while fullback Josh Schmidt took his game from the intramural fields to Notre Dame Stadium and emerged as a part-time starter in 2003. In 2007 and '08, defensive back Mike Anello earned rave reviews for his kick coverage.

66 The Touring Trophies

The Shillelaghs, Megaphone, and Co.

Another long college football tradition has involved the battle for the various traveling trophies representing certain longstanding rivalries.

Notre Dame competes for a handful of those trophies based on rivalries with USC, Purdue, Michigan State, Stanford, and Boston College.

While Notre Dame hasn't treated these traveling items quite as prominently as some schools (nowhere near the notoriety of the Indiana-Purdue Old Oaken Bucket or the Stanford-California axe), the trophies since 2008 have been housed in Notre Dame's Eck Visitors Center, headquarters of the Alumni Association, where they are part of a display.

Here's a quick primer on the hardware:

Shillelagh (USC)—To the yearly winner of Notre Dame football games against USC passes a shillelagh. According to one legend, the jeweled shillelagh awarded annually to the winner of the USC–Notre Dame clash was flown from Ireland by Howard Hughes' pilot. Emerald-studded shamrocks with the year and game score represent Notre Dame victories, while ruby-adorned Trojan heads stand for USC wins. On the end of the club is engraved, "From the Emerald Isle." The original Notre Dame–USC shillelagh, designed by Los Angeles artist John Green, was retired after the 1995 season and is on permanent display in Notre Dame's Sports Heritage Hall at the Joyce Center. A second shillelagh made its debut for the 1996 season and was acquired by Jim Gillis—a former baseball player at both Notre Dame and USC and former president of the Notre Dame Club of Los Angeles—when Notre Dame played Navy in Dublin in 1996.

Shillelagh (Purdue)—Notre Dame and Purdue also battle for a shillelagh trophy, this one donated by the late Joe McLaughlin, a merchant seaman and Notre Dame fan who brought the club from Ireland. Following each Notre Dame–Purdue contest, a football with the winner's initial and the final score is attached to the stand. The shillelagh has been the prize of the Irish-Boilermaker contests since 1957.

Megaphone (Michigan State)—The annual winner of the Notre Dame–Michigan State game receives a megaphone trophy, sponsored jointly by the Detroit alumni clubs of Notre Dame and Michigan State. The award has been presented each year since 1949. The megaphone is painted half blue (with a gold ND monogram) and half white (with a green MSU). All previous game scores are inscribed upon it, and the rivalry trophy actually now consists of three megaphones, after all the spaces were filled on the first two trophies.

Legends Trophy (Stanford)—The winner of the Notre Dame–Stanford series receives the Legends Trophy, a combination of Irish crystal and California redwood. The Notre Dame Club of the San Francisco Bay Area presented the trophy for the first time in 1989.

Leahy Bowl (Boston College)—The Frank Leahy Memorial Bowl—a crystal trophy placed on a wooden base—is presented by the Notre Dame Club of Boston to the winner of the Notre Dame–Boston College game and is named after the legendary coach who served as head coach at both Boston College and Notre Dame. Leahy led the Eagles to a 20–2–0 record in 1939 and '40 before returning to his alma mater, coaching the Irish to four national championships in 11 seasons. Notre Dame student government also created a rivalry trophy to pass between the students of Notre Dame and Boston College. The Leahy Bowl is intended to inspire a spirit of sportsmanship and friendly competition.

67 Attend a Friday Night Pep Rally

No One Else Does It Every Week

Pep rallies are an old-school college football tradition. However, Notre Dame apparently is the only school that holds one for every home football game—and has been doing so for as long as anyone can remember.

Once upon a time, Notre Dame football pep rallies were essentially internal affairs. The Old Fieldhouse, longtime middle-of-the-campus home to Irish basketball games, welcomed a crowd that predominantly featured students. Players and coaches occupied the balcony.

Eventually, the rallies moved to Stepan Center on the north edge of campus. During the Dan Devine/Gerry Faust/Lou Holtz years, the general public began showing more of an interest in rallies, and the University's fire marshal suggested a larger venue as wall-to-wall crowds overflowed Stepan.

The rallies moved to the Joyce Center field house (the ice-rink side), with attendees standing festival style. Finally, demand for access to the rally become so high—including groups like students, players' parents, benefactors, plus general fans—that the rallies moved to the Joyce Center arena with its 11,000-plus seats.

A handful of rallies have been held in Notre Dame Stadium, most of them based on anticipation of particularly high demand for seats. The first of those was held the night prior to the 1997 dedication of the renovated Notre Dame Stadium (with 35,000 attendees). The 1998 and 2000 seasons also both featured an early-season rally. The largest crowd, about 45,000 fans, gathered for the rally before the 2005 Notre Dame–USC game—with Joe Montana, Tim Brown, Chris Zorich, and Dan "Rudy" Ruettiger the featured guest speakers.

One of the first outdoor rallies came outside of Stepan Center for the 1988 Notre Dame-Miami game when Holtz predicted the Irish would win the next day (that's when Holtz later said, "No one should ever be held responsible for what they say at a pep rally").

Rallies routinely begin once the band comes into the Joyce Center a few minutes before 6:30 PM. The football team follows, to strains of the Notre Dame "Victory March." The normal speaking agenda includes several players, the head coach, and often a special guest or two. Recent guest speakers have been Regis Philbin, Dick Vitale, "Rudy" Ruettiger, Hank Aaron, Wayne Gretzky, Jon Bon Jovi, and many former players (Jerome Bettis) and coaches (Holtz, Ara Parseghian). National championship teams holding reunions are often seated on the floor beside the current team, commonly providing a speaker or two for the program.

Recent seasons have featured a handful of host dorms for each rally, meaning a half-dozen or so groups of brightly (and sometimes crazily) attired student groups sit front and center facing the football squad.

Student spirit groups often provide skits, speakers, or other pre-rally entertainment. The pom-pom squad performs, and videos were added to the program beginning in 2008.

Student seating is generally guaranteed, but the general public seating crunch proved so great in recent years that the Notre Dame ticket office began issuing tickets (good for seating in a particular

The largest crowd to attend a pep rally at the Stadium, about 45,000 fans, gathered before the 2005 Notre Dame–USC game—with Joe Montana, Tim Brown, Chris Zorich, and Dan "Rudy" Ruettiger as the featured guest speakers.

section) for Friday afternoon pickup to better control access to the Joyce Center.

Some alumni have decried that rallies aren't like they were "in the good old days." True enough. However, the growth of all that a Notre Dame football weekend involves now ensures that some 10,000 fans every single home football Friday come to fete the Fighting Irish. That doesn't happen anywhere else in America.

68 Attend a Friday Kickoff Luncheon

It's "Notre Dame Football Live"

During Ara Parseghian's tenure as Irish head coach, South Bend lawyer Charlie Sweeney started the Notre Dame Quarterback Club, a group of local businessmen who gathered at noon each Monday in the Monogram Room of the Athletic & Convocation Center. Parseghian would roll the 16-millimeter game films and explain what had happened on the previous Saturday.

Eventually, the luncheons moved to Fridays before home games and, like the pep rallies, featured guest speakers and became of greater interest to the public. The luncheons eventually outgrew the 350-seat Monogram Room and moved to the Joyce Center fieldhouse where crowds of 2,500 could attend.

The Quarterback Club eventually disbanded, and the Notre Dame athletics department took over most of the organizational structure of the events.

Like the pep rallies, the Friday kickoff luncheons benefited greatly from the motivation, humor, and speaking acumen of former Irish coach Lou Holtz. Even luncheon attendees who knew nothing about football would walk away from the event remembering some pithy line from Holtz. It was also a chance to see the personal side of Irish players and coaches.

Local sportscaster Bob Nagle currently presents the program and interviews guests from behind a desk Leno/Letterman–style.

Order forms for tickets are generally available by mid-summer on the Notre Dame athletic website at www.und.com.

69 Tour the Gug

State-of-the-Art Home to Notre Dame Football

Not so long ago, the Notre Dame football team dressed for practice in a non-descript locker room in the Joyce Center that never featured a single bit of signage or imaging that mentioned Notre Dame football.

That locker room was utilized from the time the Athletic & Convocation Center opened in 1968–69. It was anything but a stop on the tour for Irish football recruits.

The Irish took a brief detour in 1997 when the enlarged Notre Dame Stadium opened, including a doubled-in-size home team locker area that through the 2004 season was used for practices during the week in addition to Saturdays.

Then in 2005 came the Guglielmino Athletics Complex, a new state-of-the-art facility that became home to virtually the entire Notre Dame football operation.

The lobby of the Gug includes one trophy case that features the 1988 national championship trophy awarded to the Irish for finishing No. 1 in the *USA Today* poll of coaches (that's the trophy with the crystal football). A second case includes a Heisman Trophy and a listing of Notre Dame's seven winners. (The university didn't want to move any of the actual seven Heismans out of the Joyce Center display, so it worked out a deal with the Heisman Trust to lease a replica copy to house at the Gug.) In between the two cases is a sculpture of the Four Horsemen that was dedicated in 2008. The Guglielmino family felt so strongly about wanting to honor the Four Horsemen that it made the sculpture a part of its benefaction agreement with the university.

One of the finest athletic facilities in the nation, the Guglielmino Athletics Complex houses virtually the entire Notre Dame football operation.

The Gug, underwritten with a gift from the late Don F. Guglielmino and his wife Flora, provides the Notre Dame football team with one of the top facilities in the nation. The building gives the Irish football team a central location for post-practice and pre-practice routines as well as daily positional meetings. Before The Gug opened, the Irish football facilities were spread between Notre Dame Stadium, the Joyce Center, and the Loftus Sports Center.

The 96,000-square-foot complex was designed and built by McShane Construction of Chicago. Interior design and banners were produced by ZeDesign of Dayton, Ohio. Groundbreaking took place on May 5, 2004.

The first floor of the Guglielmino Complex features the 25,000-square-foot Haggar Fitness Center (gift of Ed and Patty Haggar and Joe and Isabell Haggar) with the latest state-of-the-art equipment that all student-athletes can use on a daily basis. The 8,300-square-foot Loftus Sports Medicine and Rehabilitation Center (a gift of John and Julie Loftus) services all of Notre Dame's student-athletes. The athletic training facility is a state-of-the-art area with two new swim exercise pools—one of which includes a treadmill at the bottom. The facility also houses the athletic training staff and gives that department significant office space in addition to increased area for rehabilitation.

Also located on the first floor is the Allen Equipment Room (a gift of Marty and Sue Allen), which houses the football equipment staff and storage facility used for both practices and competition.

The Haggar Fitness Center is perhaps the most eye-catching feature of the Gug, as the previous fitness center has been expanded to twice its size. The Haggar Fitness Center is shared by both the Guglielmino Complex and the Loftus Center and services all of Notre Dame's 26 varsity athletic sports.

The fitness complex features more than 250 pieces of weight-training equipment, six plasma television screens, a state-of-the-art sound system, a 50-yard track for speed workouts and a 45 x 18-yard Prestige Turf field for team stretching exercises and workouts.

The Romano Family Locker Room (a gift of D.J. "Buddy" and Florence Romano) provides the players instant access to the practice fields, fitness center, and Loftus. The locker room houses 125 spacious (49x90) lockers with shoe warmers/driers, 22 showers, a "mud room," and a players' lounge that includes a 52-inch plasma TV and kitchen.

Adjacent to the players' locker room is the Hickey Coaches' Locker Room (a gift of Jack and Rosemary Hickey) that includes 20 spacious lockers and six private showers.

The Isban Auditorium (a gift of Leonard and JoAnn Isban) measures 3,800 square feet with 150 theater-style, football-player-sized seats and theater-quality audio-visual equipment, including a 30-foot screen.

The second floor houses the Smith Family Office Suites (gift of the Smith family in honor of Francis W. and Rita C. Smith) in a 7,800-square-foot area, with head coach Charlie Weis' area overlooking the Cartier Field practice complex.

The assistant coaches are arranged along offensive and defensive hallways, while the video coordinator's compound sits in the center of the coaches' offices and is linked into every room in the building. There is also a recruiting lounge on the second floor, which features a balcony overlooking the strength and conditioning complex and a panoramic window with a view of Notre Dame's central campus. The head coach's suite is located at the far southern tip on the second floor of the Guglielmino Athletics Complex. Weis has a large reception area, a private bathroom, shower facility, and two offices—one for official meetings and another private area for film work.

The Morse Recruiting Lounge (a gift of Jim and Leah Morse) is one of the signature features of the Gug. Located on the second floor above the main entrance, the recruiting lounge offers a beautiful view of campus and a glimpse of Notre Dame's football excellence—11 national championship banners hang in the room to commemorate Notre Dame's 11 consensus national titles. The recruiting lounge offers a balcony glimpse of the signature two-story mural near the main entrance of the Guglielmino Athletics Complex.

The aforementioned mural is just one of several graphic presentations in the Gug. Along with the stunning two-story mural, there are displays honoring Notre Dame's national championships, Heisman Trophy winners, All-Americans, walk-ons, and players currently in the NFL.

After the death of his father, Guglielmino transferred to Stanford University in 1940 due to pressing family needs. He then left school to enlist in the Army Air Corps and serve in the Pacific theatre during World War II. After the war, Guglielmino returned to his hometown of Glendale, California, where he became a successful businessman. He founded Newhall Hardware Company in 1947 and helped found the Santa Clarita National Bank in the mid-1960s. He served as the bank's chairman of the board until it was sold, first to Security Pacific National Bank in 1990 and later to Bank of America.

70 Edward "Moose" Krause

A Man for All Seasons at Notre Dame

Fans who enjoy strolling the Notre Dame campus during a football weekend have a new site to add to their agenda, as a bronze sculpture of legendary Irish student-athlete, head coach, and athletic director Edward "Moose" Krause has been placed in front of the Joyce Center, looking over at Notre Dame Stadium.

The sculpture—dedicated on September 17, 1999, the day before Notre Dame played host to Michigan State—shows Krause sitting on a bench, looking toward Notre Dame Stadium. It was produced by Jerry McKenna of Boerne, Texas, a 1962 Notre Dame graduate who previously produced the Frank Leahy sculpture that was unveiled in the fall of 1997 outside of Notre Dame Stadium. He later did the Ara Parseghian and Lou Holtz sculptures, as well.

Krause's many honors included being inducted into the Knights of Malta—the highest honor a layman can receive in the Catholic church—at ceremonies conducted in New York's St.

Patrick's Cathedral by Cardinal Terence Cook. The City of Hope National Medical Center honored Krause in 1997 and established an Edward Krause Research Fellowship in recognition of his service to that organization's philanthropic interests.

Krause was named Man of the Year by the Walter Camp Football Foundation for his lifetime achievements and received the 1989 Distinguished American Award from the National Football Foundation and Hall of Fame. He served as the University Division representative for district four of the National Association of College Directors of Athletics and was elected to the Honors Court of the NCAA, in addition to serving on the National Football Foundation and Hall of Fame honors court.

He earned three football monograms as a tackle at Notre Dame in 1931, '32 and '33, in addition to earning All-America honors in '32. But his biggest college athletic heroics were accomplished on the basketball court as a center, and he was inducted into the Naismith Basketball Hall of Fame in 1976. Krause earned All-America honors in both basketball and football and also earned a monogram in track. After graduating in 1934, Krause returned to Notre Dame in 1942 as an assistant basketball and football coach. When his former mentor George Keogan died of a heart attack during the 1942–43 season, Krause finished the season as the head basketball coach and served in that same capacity the following season, followed by five seasons as the Irish head coach.

Krause was appointed assistant athletic director at Notre Dame in 1948 and became the Notre Dame athletic director on March 22, 1949, a position that he held until retiring in 1980 after 32 years on the job. During Krause's tenure, the Notre Dame football team played in nine bowl games and won four consensus national championships. The basketball team advanced to the NCAA Final Four in 1978 and made 16 appearances in the NCAA tournament. Krause helped spearhead the building of the multipurpose Joyce

Longtime athletics director Moose Krause was immortalized in this sculpture by Jerry McKenna that sits in front of the Joyce Center.

Center, which opened in 1968, with a fund-raising tour which saw him visit 175 cities. He also saw 10 new sports reach varsity status at Notre Dame and handled the establishment of women's varsity sports beginning in 1974.

Krause passed away on December 11, 1992, one day after attending the Notre Dame athletic department Christmas party and just weeks before he planned on attending Notre Dame's appearance in the 1993 Cotton Bowl.

If Notre Dame athletics ever had a more effective long-term ambassador than Krause, it would be hard to identify that individual.

71 Mario "Motts" Tonelli

A True Irish Hero

Former Notre Dame running back Mario "Motts" Tonelli, a native of Skokie, Illinois, received the University's 2000 Rev. William Corby Award for distinguished military service by a Notre Dame graduate.

Mario Tonelli played fullback with the Irish in the mid-1930s. A soldier in World War II, he survived the Bataan Death March, was a prisoner of war, and returned home to embark on a career in politics.

Tonelli was a fullback with the Irish in the mid-1930s and later survived the infamous Bataan Death March, spending 42 months as a prisoner of war before embarking on a distinguished career in Chicago politics. In March 2002, he was inducted into the National Italian-American Sports Hall of Fame.

Tonelli, who also played professional football briefly with the Chicago Cardinals, passed away on January 7, 2003. His fascinating life story received national attention, including a *USA Today* feature story and an in-depth feature that ran in *Sports Illustrated* just weeks after his death.

Snow Bowl

The 1992 Penn State Game

The 1992 Notre Dame–Penn State contest in Notre Dame Stadium merited the attention of Irish fans for a handful of reasons:

- It marked the final home appearance of an impressive cadre of players, notably Rick Mirer, Jerome Bettis, and Reggie Brooks.
- It marked the final scheduled meeting between the two historic programs, mostly due to Penn State's impending entrance into the Big Ten Conference.
- It marked a bizarre weather day in South Bend, with a memorable snowstorm during parts of the contest making for some artistic photos from the event.

More than anything, the 17–16 Irish victory featured a downright amazing ending.

A mostly defensive struggle left the teams tied 6–6 at the half. From a 9–9 tie late in the fourth quarter, the No. 22 Nittany Lions took advantage of an Irish fumble to drive 44 yards for a Brian O'Neal scoring run with 4:25 on the clock to give Penn State a 16–9 lead.

The eighth-rated and once-beaten Irish took over at the Penn State 36 and made great use of three plays—a 21-yard gain when Mirer threw to Bettis, a 14-yard run by Mirer, and a Mirer-to-Ray Griggs connection for 17 more.

It finally came down to fourth down and goal from the Penn State 3-yard line with 25 seconds left. Mirer found Bettis in the end zone to make it 16–15.

That left the Irish to attempt a two-pointer. Mirer had hoped to find his tight end, but he ended up scrambling to his right—and Brooks ran from the left side through the back of the end zone toward the right corner.

Brooks had to lay out almost horizontal to get his hands on Mirer's throw—then he managed to get his feet in bounds for the two points and the Irish victory.

It was an unlikely ending for Brooks whose entire Notre Dame career had featured only two pass receptions.

73 The Wisdom of Ziggy

He'd Always Leave You Laughing

Understand first of all that Zygmont Pierre (Ziggy) Czarobski was one talented football player for Notre Dame.

He started at right tackle for the Irish in 1943, '46 and '47, helping Notre Dame to national titles in 1943 and '46 and earning first-team All-America honors from several selectors as a senior in '47. The National Football Foundation inducted him into the College Football Hall of Fame in 1977.

That being said, Czarobski also more than earned his reputation as team humorist—he became a highly popular pep-rally speaker—providing an interesting foil to taskmaster head coach Frank Leahy.

Leahy once wondered why Ziggy had showered before practice began. Czarobski quickly countered that the showers were too crowded after practice.

On a road trip, Ziggy met General Omar Bradley in a New York hotel elevator. Bradley told Czarobski how much he enjoyed Notre Dame football games. So Ziggy promptly returned the compliment, telling Bradley how much all the Irish players enjoyed Bradley's battles.

Frustrated with his team's struggles, Leahy decided a return to fundamentals might be in order—so he held up a ball and stated, "Gentlemen, this is a football."

Ziggy's immediate retort was, "Not so fast, Coach!"

74 Catch a Glimpse of Terri Buck

Notre Dame's All-America Cheerleader

For the record, Notre Dame first admitted women in 1972, and today females comprise about half (47 percent) of Notre Dame's undergraduate population of 8,363 (based on 2008–09 enrollment). Before that, Saint Mary's College students comprised the female portion of the Notre Dame cheerleading squad.

And so it was that Terri Buck arguably became the most famous cheerleader in Notre Dame history. Buck's good looks earned her cover-girl status on the Notre Dame football pocket schedule cards in 1971—a spot normally reserved for football stars like Joe Theismann.

A series of five Buck photos in cheerleader uniform also appeared that year on the back cover of the Notre Dame Football Guide—once again, in a spot normally reserved for players.

It's noteworthy that Irish coach Ara Parseghian appeared on the front cover of that '71 media guide. Neither he nor Buck required identification.

Buck, who came from Morgan Hill, California, had an older brother and a cousin who attended Notre Dame. She recalls that, in the absence of women at Notre Dame, the university determined her freshman year at Saint Mary's to have female cheerleaders from Saint Mary's. Buck says about 30 women tried out—and four were selected—and the rest is history.

After Buck graduated, she married former Irish walk-on football player Brian Lewallen (a 1970 graduate), and they now live in Palos Verdes Estates, California, where they are parents of five children.

She remains the gold standard when it comes to Notre Dame cheerleading.

75 "This is Sergeant Tim McCarthy for the Indiana State Police"

Game Tradition Rates Legendary Status

Once upon a time, Tim McCarthy was an Indiana State Police sergeant from Michigan City, Indiana, who was assigned to work most Notre Dame home football games. In the early 1960s, the State

"Remember, if you drive to beat the band, you may have to face the music." Officer Tim McCarthy's public safety messages early in the fourth quarter have been a home game tradition at Notre Dame since the early 1960s.

Police proactively decided to offer a safety message during Irish home games, and they assigned McCarthy to the task.

McCarthy decided to add a dash of humor and wit to the message, and each Saturday he came up with some sort of pun that had to do with driving and drinking—and sometimes a combination of the two.

In the early days, McCarthy's messages didn't create much of a stir. But eventually his public-address announcements, placed early in the fourth period each Saturday, drew something of a cult following among Irish fans.

For years, no one even knew what McCarthy looked like. He would sit innocuously in the Notre Dame Stadium press box—and then make his way to the public-address booth at his assigned time.

Once he retired and no longer wore a uniform, he became even harder to spot.

But by then McCarthy had become part of the lore of Notre Dame football game experiences. His safety messages became so anticipated that when McCarthy delivered his opening line, "This is Tim McCarthy for the Indiana State Police." the crowd let loose with a roar that would rival any heard all day in Notre Dame's venerable home facility.

Naturally, some of McCarthy's messages are cleverer than others, but they never cease to inspire a reaction from fans at the Irish games. The "groan quotient" can be measured audibly on a Saturday-to-Saturday basis.

As the years rolled by, McCarthy's star status grew. Once only a voice from on high in the press box, suddenly McCarthy found himself in demand. He was featured in a 1990 coffee-table photo book about Notre Dame football. He was invited to appear at Notre Dame pep rallies, the Irish football banquet, and the Friday kickoff luncheons. He's been featured in the Notre Dame football game program and in various newspapers and magazines, as well.

In 2006, McCarthy and the Notre Dame Band of the Fighting Irish collaborated on a CD offering that featured 15 of his safety messages, interspersed with traditional Notre Dame school songs. Titled "May I Have Your Attention Please," the CD included the reminder, "Remember, if you drive to beat the band, you may have to face the music."

At this writing, McCarthy and longtime Notre Dame Stadium public-address announcer Mike Collins are collaborating on a book that will detail the growth of McCarthy's career as the resident humorist/safety lecturer of Notre Dame football. The book will include every message ever delivered by McCarthy in Notre Dame's stadium (he keeps them all on index cards).

76 Lindsey Nelson and the C.D. Chesley Company

"And Now We Move to Further Action in the Third Period"

Knute Rockne remains the winningest coach in the history of college football from a percentage standpoint. Right behind him is Frank Leahy. Between them they won seven consensus national championships.

However, despite the successes of Notre Dame football coaches like Rockne and Leahy—not to mention the exploits of the 45 Irish players now enshrined in the College Football Hall of Fame—the two individuals who may have done more for the marketing of Notre Dame football than anyone else are C.D. Chesley and Lindsey Nelson.

Back in the fledgling days of television, Chesley did a deal with Notre Dame that gave him the ability to show a one-hour replay of every Irish football game on Sunday mornings beginning with the 1964 season. With precious few college games aired live, and with the growing interest in Notre Dame's program, the Sunday morning telecasts became staples of life in the fall for millions of sports fans. And the timing of the replays in various markets around the country assuredly impacted church attendance among oft-times conflicted worshippers.

Nelson handled the play-by-play description of the replayed games for years. Because the games had to be edited down and could not include every series, Nelson became as well known for his classic segue phrases—"And now we move to further action in the third period"—as maybe anything else he ever uttered in his career.

The replays actually began in 1959, with WNDU-TV in South Bend producing the shows and United Press International distributing the games to 60 stations (WGN-TV in Chicago took over that role starting in 1960). Harry Wismer and Moose Krause were the original commentators. When Chesley took over in 1964, he assigned Nelson and Paul Hornung to the broadcasts.

George Connor replaced Hornung in 1978, Metrosports took over the replays from Chesley in 1980, and Lou Boda spent one year in the play-by-play role in 1980. Harry Kalas called the games from '81 through '84—and the project ended after the '84 season (the same year the Supreme Court ruled against the NCAA in the television rights suit brought by Georgia and Oklahoma, thus eliminating the Notre Dame replays in favor of live televised games every Saturday).

77 Rocky Bleier

A Distinguished American Indeed

Bob "Rocky" Bleier never qualified as a superstar running back during his days as a Notre Dame football player.

However, his football exploits with the Irish and the Pittsburgh Steelers, combined with his military and other off-the-field contributions, earned him the 2007 Distinguished American Award from the National Football Foundation.

The Distinguished American Award is presented by the NFF on special occasions when a truly deserving individual emerges. The award honors someone who has applied the character-building attributes learned from amateur football in their business and personal life, exhibiting superior leadership qualities in education, amateur athletics, business, and in the community.

Notre Dame running back Rocky Bleier retired from the NFL as a four-time Super Bowl champion.

Bleier joined a list of previous winners that included Vince Lombardi, Bob Hope, Pete Rozelle, and the late Pat Tillman. Other previous winners with Notre Dame connections include former Notre Dame president Rev. Theodore M. Hesburgh, C.S.C. (1975); former Notre Dame executive vice president Rev. Edmund P. Joyce, C.S.C. (1977); former Notre Dame athletics director Edward "Moose" Krause (1989); University trustee and Elkhart, Indiana, businessman Art Decio (2000); and former Irish football All-American Alan Page (2005).

A football and basketball star in Appleton, Wisconsin, Bleier attended Notre Dame as a standout running back for the Irish under Hall of Fame coach Ara Parseghian. He received his degree in business management in 1968.

Bleier then played one season in the NFL before being drafted by the U.S. Army to fight in Vietnam. While serving in 1969, Bleier's platoon was ambushed and his left thigh was wounded. Additionally, a grenade sent pieces of shrapnel into his right leg while he was down. His courageous service earned him the Purple Heart and the Bronze Star. Bleier returned to the pros in 1970, but he played only sparingly for the Pittsburgh Steelers over the next three seasons. He not only needed to gain a great deal of weight back, but his war injuries made it difficult for him to walk. Through perseverance and a strict training regimen, Bleier worked his way into a starting spot in 1974. He would retire from the NFL as a four-time Super Bowl champion.

Bleier wrote a book called *Fighting Back: The Rocky Bleier Story*, which depicted his struggle to recuperate following Vietnam. He also established Rocky Bleier Inc. in 1980, serving as a motivational speaker worldwide. His speech, "Be the Best You Can Be," encourages audiences to keep on striving for greater accomplishments. He still resides in Pittsburgh, Pennsylvania.

78 Daryle Lamonica

From South Bend to AFL Legend

When the subject of Notre Dame quarterbacks comes up, Daryle Lamonica is generally not the first name that comes to mind. Lamonica suffered in terms of recognition and publicity from playing during one of the least-successful eras of Irish football (he started for Notre Dame in 1960, '61 and '62 when his teams combined for 12 wins against 18 losses).

However, Lamonica—though he seldom draws comparisons to Joe Montana or Joe Theismann or even Angelo Bertelli or John Lujack before him—made his own mark in an Irish uniform and then became one of the most amazing passers in the history of the gun-slinging American Football League.

First, Lamonica won third-team All-America honors as a senior in 1962 from the Associated Press. That year he completed 64-of-128 throws for 821 yards and six touchdowns.

Next, Lamonica joined the pre-merger AFL version of the Buffalo Bills, playing in an era of wide-open offense and pass-happy play-calling. Despite qualifying as only a 24th-round AFL and 12th-round NFL draft selection, Lamonica played for the Bills from 1963–66, then with the Oakland Raiders from 1967–74. He threw 30 touchdown passes in 1967, 34 more in 1969, and earned AFL MVP honors both seasons. He helped Buffalo to AFL titles in 1964 and '65 and Oakland in '67. A five-time Pro Bowl selection, Lamonica threw for 19,154 career yards and 164 touchdowns in his professional career.

The Kick

Harry Oliver's 51-Yard Field Goal in 1980

Take a poll of the most memorable plays in Notre Dame football history and you'll get a bunch of votes for the 51-yard field goal launched by Harry Oliver in 1980 to beat Michigan as time ran out.

Why?

At a time when television had not yet come to dominate the landscape, Tony Roberts' radio play-by-play call on Notre Dame's Westwood One network might well rank as his most famous of all time.

Then there was a now-famous black-and-white photograph (yes, black and white) that perfectly captured Oliver's follow-through as a Michigan defender tried vainly to reach the football. In a day when the Notre Dame Stadium press box barely contained enough room for the media, Fathers Ted Hesburgh and Ned Joyce (then University president and executive vice president) can be seen (in sunglasses) about a dozen rows up in the seats in the background of the photo. Undergraduate photographer Peter Romzick (he was shooting for the *Dome*, Notre Dame's yearbook) snapped the photo.

Though Oliver died in 2007 of stomach cancer, holder Tim Koegel, also an Irish backup quarterback, has spent countless hours (and settled who knows how many bets) recounting exactly how the wind stopped blowing at exactly the right moment to give Oliver's attempt a better chance to clear the uprights.

Oliver's memorable left-footed, soccer-style kick remains one of the longest ever by a Notre Dame player (at any point in a game) and represents one of only seven times in the program's 122-year history that the Irish have won on the final play of regulation. Despite having attempted only one previous field goal in a Notre Dame varsity game, Oliver was up to the task in the waning seconds versus Michigan and went on to have a record-setting junior season in 1980 that included making 18-of-23 field goals, highlighted by two different games when he sent four through the uprights (tying what was then the Irish single-game record).

An accomplished student who majored in mechanical engineering, Oliver ultimately became an engineer in the construction business, served since 1988 as a senior estimator/project manager with Cincinnati-based Performance Contracting, and later owned a real estate company. Many of his construction projects were geared toward assisting charitable organizations and schools in southern Ohio.

Both teams seemingly won that 1980 Irish-Wolverine clash in the final minutes. Notre Dame's Phil Carter smashed over from four yards for his second touchdown of the game, giving the Irish a 26–21 lead that would have been 28–21 (if not for a missed PAT by Oliver and later a failed two-point try).

Michigan's Butch Woolfolk answered on the next drive with a pair of draw plays that gained 57 yards—and the Wolverines went on to crack the end zone with just 41 ticks left on the clock (27–26).

Notre Dame freshman Blair Kiel then drove the Irish downfield, leaving the ball on the Michigan 34-yard line with only 0:04 remaining on the clock.

All of the drama up to that point was more than enough to provide the most fantastic of finishes. But it's always better when Mother Nature gets involved. In this case, Oliver took the field with a brisk 15 mile-an-hour wind in his face as he eyed the goalposts in the south end zone.

"I just remember thinking this wind is very strong and half-thinking I don't have a chance in heck of making this thing," Oliver would later say.

But then, the unthinkable happened—a meteorological shift occurred in which many observers claim that the wind suddenly stepped aside to complement the hushed tone amidst a crowd of nearly 60,000. Michigan's outside rushers crashed in for the attempted block—and one of those players knocked Oliver down and he never saw the ball clear the crossbar (by inches).

Although the Notre Dame media guide and record supplements do not usually include complete listings for the longest field goals in the program's history, there are nine different kickers listed among the top-12 leaders for single-season field goals and none of them ever recorded a boot of more than 51 yards (Nicholas Setta and Dave Reeve each had a long of 51). And when looking at the six other Notre Dame games that have ended with a win on the final play of regulation, the longest kick was the 41-yarder by Joe Perkowski to beat Syracuse in 1961 (17–15).

The other four kickers who have won Notre Dame games as the final whistle sounded include: Carney (19-yarder at USC in 1986, 38–37); Jim Sanson (38-yarder at Texas in 1996, 27–24); Setta (38-yarder at home vs. Purdue in 2000, 23–21); and D.J. Fitzpatrick (40-yarder vs. Navy in 2003, 27–24). Carney and Setta's kicks both came with the Irish trailing, while Sanson and Fitzpatrick lined up their kicks with a tie score on the board. The only other Notre Dame win on the final play was in the Cotton Bowl following the 1978 season, when Joe Montana's eight-yard pass to Kris Haines and the ensuing extra point from Joe Unis capped a furious 35–34 comeback.

There are 53 documented games in which Notre Dame scored the ultimate winning or tying points in the final 5:00—but very few of them covered at least half of the field, as did Oliver's kick. In fact, only three other fantastic finishes in Notre Dame history have seen the clinching late play cover more than 50 yards: the 80-yard pass play between Montana and Ted Burgmeier in the 1975 win over North Carolina (1:03 left, 21–14); a similar 67-yard run-and-catch involving Carlyle Holiday and Omar Jenkins, vs. Navy in 2002 (2:08, 30–23); and the short slant pass from Pat Dillingham to Arnaz Battle that turned into a 60-yard touchdown for the decisive points in the 2002 win at Michigan State (1:15, 21–17).

80 Stroll Through Heritage Hall

A Walk Down Notre Dame's Athletics Memory Lane

Newly renovated Heritage Hall, where the history of Notre Dame athletics program is on display, re-opened in September 2008 on the second-floor concourse of the Joyce Center.

The Notre Dame Monogram Club allocated more than $600,000 for the improvements to Heritage Hall, which originally opened in 1988.

There are multiple display cases dedicated to each of Notre Dame's 26 varsity sports, plus special areas to recognize Notre Dame's 27 national championships and national award winners. An additional display lists all of Notre Dame's first- and second-team All-Americans, as well as Academic All-America selections and NCAA Post-Graduate Scholarship winners. That same display features 20 of the most accomplished Notre Dame student-athletes.

Also part of the renovations are displays highlighting sports like wrestling and field hockey that are no longer varsity offerings, plus cases highlighting Monogram Club leadership and awards, Notre Dame Stadium, Notre Dame's walk-on tradition, RecSports, cheerleaders and mascots, athletic trainers and student managers, student welfare and development, the O.S.C.A.R.S, former University executive vice-president Rev. Edmund P. Joyce, C.S.C., and the Notre Dame band.

Additional display cases outside the entrance to the athletic administrative offices featured Notre Dame's 2008 participation in the NCAA Hockey Frozen Four, Notre Dame's 2008 swimming anniversary celebration (50 years for men, 25 for women), athletic facilities, Notre Dame's athletic/academic tradition—plus photos of all of Notre Dame's athletics directors.

Additional new displays featuring men's and women's basketball can be seen in the hallway between Gates 1 and 2 of the Joyce Center—adjacent to the basketball offices. In addition, there are new displays in the Monogram Room at the east end of the concourse that feature tributes to each of Notre Dame's 27 national championship teams representing all sports.

Football displays on the concourse include an extensive historical timeline, along with cases devoted to Knute Rockne, uniforms, Irish mystique, Notre Dame on the silver screen, historical memorabilia, Notre Dame players and coaches in the Hall of Fame, and bowl games. Also on display, as part of the national awards section, are all seven Heisman Trophies.

The displays were produced by 1220 Exhibits Inc. (manufacturing and installation) of Nashville, Tennessee, Chicago, Illinois, and Las Vegas, Nevada—and Gallagher & Associates (design group) of Bethesda, Maryland, and San Francisco, California.

Back in September 1988, the Notre Dame Monogram Club presented to the university the original Sports Heritage Hall. Those displays were organized by decade and included not only the names of every monogram winner from every sport but also a collection of photographs, trophies, and other memorabilia. A display area at the west end of the hall featured photos of Notre Dame All-Americans, Academic All-Americans, and recent awards—plus an interactive kiosk with data on all former and current monogram winners, and an elaborate searching mechanism. The hall's many national championship and bowl trophies also originally included all seven Heisman Trophies won by Notre Dame players.

In 1998, additional display cases were installed by the Monogram Club on the first floor of the Joyce Center between the football and men's basketball offices to highlight the most recent accomplishments by Irish athletes.

81 The Alma Mater

Part of Irish Football Tradition

Composed by Joseph J. Casasanta (a 1923 Notre Dame graduate), "Notre Dame, Our Mother" has been the alma mater of the University since it was written for the 1930 dedication of Notre Dame Stadium. Written in honor of the University's patron, Blessed Virgin Mary, the song is part of the halftime show of the Band of the Fighting Irish and is the traditional conclusion to Notre Dame pep rallies.

Following his first season in 2005 as coach at Notre Dame, Charlie Weis originated a tradition that now has the entire Irish team singing the alma mater with the band in front of the Notre Dame student section following each Irish home game.

Notre Dame, Our Mother, Tender, strong and true,
Proudly in the heavens, Gleams the Gold and Blue,
Glory's mantle cloaks thee, Golden is thy fame,
And our hearts forever, Praise thee, Notre Dame.
And our hearts forever, Love thee, Notre Dame.

82 The "Other" Irish Hall of Famers

Seven Rockne-Era Notre Dame Players Inducted as Coaches

There's no shortage of Notre Dame representation in the National Football Foundation's College Football Hall of Fame that's housed in downtown South Bend.

In fact, Notre Dame has more inductees than any other school—with 42 former Irish players and six former Irish head coaches on the list. The most recent selections have included Lou Holtz (2008), Chris Zorich (2007), John Huarte (2005), and Joe Theismann (2004).

In addition—and assuredly not as well known—there are seven former Notre Dame football players who have been inducted into the College Football Hall of Fame as coaches, with all of them having played with or for Knute Rockne while in South Bend.

Eddie Anderson

He played at Notre Dame 1918–21 ('21 Irish captain and consensus All-American end); head coach at Loras (1922–24, 16–6–1 record), DePaul (1925–32, 21–22–3), Holy Cross (1933–38, 47–7–4), Iowa (1939–42 and 1946–49, 35–33–2) and again at Holy Cross (1950–64, 82–60–4); 39-year career record of 201–128–15 (.606) made him only the fourth college football coach to win 200 games; inducted into the Hall of Fame in 1971.

Anderson's last three teams at Notre Dame (1919–21) produced a combined 28–1 record with the Mason City, Iowa, product losing only to home-state rival Iowa, 10–7, in 1921. He also played on the 1925 Chicago Cardinal team that won the NFL title. He graduated from medical school while coaching at DePaul, then left for Holy Cross where he produced unbeaten seasons in 1935 and '37 (and his 1937 and '38 Holy Cross teams finished 14th and ninth, respectively, in the final AP poll).

In 1939—his first season at Iowa—Anderson earned national Coach of the Year honors after guiding Heisman Trophy winner Nile Kinnick and the Hawks to a 6–1–1 record (Iowa fans gave him a Cadillac as a reward). When he left Iowa to serve n the Army medical corps during World War II, he was succeeded for the next two seasons by another former Note Dame player, Slip Madigan.

Anderson's 1951 Holy Cross team ended up 8–2 and No. 19 in the AP rankings. Following his resignation from Holy Cross, he became the chief of outpatient services at the Veterans Administration Medical Center in Rutland, Massachusetts.

Charlie Bachman

He played at Notre Dame 1914–16 (second-team All-American guard in '16); head coach at Northwestern (1919, 2–5 record), Kansas State (1920–27, 33–23–9), Florida (1928–32, 27–18–3), and Michigan State (1933–42 and 1944–46, 70–34–10); 27-year career record of 132–80–22 (.611); inducted into the Hall of Fame in 1978.

After leaving Notre Dame, Bachman played for Great Lakes Naval Station in 1918 and helped his team finish 7–0–2 (including a tie against Notre Dame) and play in the Rose Bowl.

At Kansas State in 1924 his Wildcats defeated rival Kansas for the first time in 18 years. Then at Michigan State, his Spartans defeated rival Michigan in four straight seasons (1934–37) after 18 straight defeats to the Wolverines. His 1937 Spartan team finished 8–2 and played in the Orange Bowl.

Harry Baujan

He played at Notre Dame 1913–16 (starter at end in '15 and '16); head coach at Dayton (1923–46, 124–64–8 record, .653); inducted into the Hall of Fame in 1990.

Baujan coached the Dayton men's basketball team from 1923–28 and also served as athletics director at Dayton. Baujan Field at Dayton is the current home of the Flyer soccer teams (built in 1925 for football, named in Baujan's honor in 1961).

Gus Dorais

He played at Notre Dame 1910–13 (four-year starter at quarterback, consensus first-team All-American in '13); head coach at Columbia (now Loras, 1914–17, 17–9–2 record), Gonzaga (1920–24, 20–13–4) and Detroit (1925–42, 113–48–7); 27-year career record of 150–70–13 (.671); head coach of NFL Detroit Lions (1943–47, 20–31–2); inducted into the Hall of Fame in 1954.

Dorais (he also served as Notre Dame's place-kicker) and Rockne (they roomed together as players) combined for the first great pass-and-catch combination in Notre Dame history, including the well-documented 35–13 win over highly regarded Army in 1913 at West Point.

In 1937, Dorais coached the college seniors—including quarterback Sammy Baugh—to a 6–0 win over the NFL champion Green Bay Packers (the first time the college players had ever beaten the pros).

Slip Madigan

He played at Notre Dame 1916, 1917–19 (starter at guard in '17, also played center); head coach at Saint Mary's (1921–39, 117–45–12 record), Iowa (1943–44, 2–13–1); 21-year career record of 119–58–13 (.660); inducted into the Hall of Fame in 1974.

Madigan developed a powerhouse program at Saint Mary's, defeating Rose Bowl–bound teams from Stanford in 1927 and USC in '31. In 1930 the Gaels ended Fordham's 16-game winning streak. In 1938 the Gaels defeated Texas Tech in the Cotton Bowl.

James Phelan

He played at Notre Dame 1915–17 ('17 Irish captain and three-year starter at quarterback); head coach at Missouri (1920–22, 13–3 record), Purdue (1922–29, 35–22–5), Washington (1930–41, 65–37–8), and Saint Mary's (1942–47, 24–25–1); 28-year career record of 137–87–14 (.605); inducted into the Hall of Fame in 1973.

Phelan's final team at Purdue in 1929 finished 8–0 and won the Big Ten title. His 1936 Washington squad went 7–2–1, won the Pacific Coast Conference crown, played in the Rose Bowl, and ended up fifth in the final AP poll. His 1940 Washington unit was 7–2 and 10th in the final AP ratings.

At Saint Mary's, his 1945 and '46 teams finished 7–2 and 6–3 and played in the Sugar Bowl and Oil Bowl, respectively.

Buck Shaw

He played at Notre Dame 1919–21 (second-team All-American tackle in '21; also was the place-kicker); head coach at North Carolina State (1924, 2–6–2 record), Santa Clara (1936–42, 47–10–4), California (1945, 4–5–1), and Air Force (1956–57, 9–8–2); 11-year career record of 62–29–8 (.666); head coach of San Francisco 49ers (1946–49 in AAFC, 38–14–2, and 1950–54 in NFL, 33–25–2) and Philadelphia Eagles (1958–60, 20–16–1, including 1960 NFL title); inducted into the Hall of Fame in 1972.

Shaw made a name for himself as a standout on Rockne's first unbeaten Notre Dame team (he originally enrolled at Creighton and had transferred to Notre Dame to compete in track). His first two Santa Clara teams in 1936 and '37 finished a combined 18–1 and defeated LSU in the Sugar Bowl both years. In 1956, he became the first-ever head coach at Air Force.

Shaw became the San Francisco 49ers first head coach in 1946 in the new All-America Football Conference. Among the players he coached there were Hugh McElhenny, Y.A. Tittle, and Frankie Albert. In his final game as a coach, Shaw and Eagle quarterback Norm Van Brocklin defeated Vince Lombardi's Green Bay Packers in the 1960 NFL Championship Game (Lombardi's only defeat in six appearances in the league title game). His predecessor as Eagles head coach was Hugh Devore, Notre Dame's head coach in 1945 and '63.

Still in operation at Santa Clara, Buck Shaw Stadium (dedicated in 1962) has been home to Bronco teams in football, baseball, and soccer.

Honorable Mention: Tom Beck

Yet another College Hall of Fame coaching inductee with a Notre Dame connection is Tom Beck, who coached the Irish running backs in 1991 under Lou Holtz. He was inducted in 2004 after serving as head coach at Benedictine (1970–74, 37–12–1 record), Elmhurst (1976–83, 50–22), and Grand Valley State (1985–90, 50–18), compiling a 137–52–1 (.723) career record.

83 Joe Boland/Westwood One/ISP

A Long History for the Irish on Radio

As Notre Dame's athletics administration several years ago researched its options for moving forward with its football radio broadcasts, it learned an interesting fact. Even ultra-successful programs like USC, Texas, and Florida had no out-of-state radio network affiliates—presumably making the Irish the only collegiate program with a truly national radio network.

Armed with that knowledge, Notre Dame and ISP Sports moved forward in 2008 with a new, 10-year business partnership in which ISP became the new exclusive national rights-holder for Notre Dame football radio broadcasts.

The Notre Dame–ISP relationship will extend through the 2017 season—with ISP managing, producing, and syndicating Notre Dame's national football radio network. In addition, the Irish broadcasts are carried via Sirius Satellite Radio—and by Notre Dame's campus radio outlet, WVFI (a web-only broadcast).

ISP, the largest collegiate-only sports marketing firm in the country, represents athletics marketing and multi-media rights for more than 40 Division I-A universities, five major conferences (including two Bowl Championship Series conferences, the Big East Conference, and the Atlantic Coast Conference) and two post-season football bowl games.

ISP took over for Westwood One, which had held Irish football radio rights since 1968, originally as the Mutual Broadcasting Company.

ISP's team of more than 250 professional sales people dedicated to the collegiate market helps maintain relationships with more than 800 radio stations (and more than 100 television stations) around the country.

Headquartered in Winston-Salem, North Carolina, ISP has nearly 50 sales offices around the country. Sutton founded the company in 1992. Among ISP clients are seven ACC athletic programs (Boston College, Clemson, Florida State, Georgia Tech, Miami, Virginia Tech, Wake Forest), five from the Big East (Cincinnati, Pittsburgh, South Florida, Syracuse, Villanova), five from the Southeastern Conference (Alabama, Auburn, Georgia, South Carolina, Vanderbilt) and three from the Pacific–10 Conference (California, UCLA, Washington). In 2007, the Big East Conference and ISP announced a six-year agreement involving virtually all conference marketing and sales.

Thus, Notre Dame remains the only college football program to have its games broadcast on a truly national radio network of linear stations. Joe Boland, former sports director at WSBT in South Bend, originated the Irish Football Network in 1948. In 1956, the Mutual Broadcasting System first carried Notre Dame games on approximately 560 stations. From 1958–67, the ABC Radio Network carried Irish games on a similar-sized network. Mutual began carrying Notre Dame games again in 1968 (that year with 253 affiliates). Mutual eventually became Westwood One (now a publicly held company managed and partly owned by CBS Radio).

Longtime radio and television play-by-play veteran Don Criqui has been the voice of Irish radio broadcasts since 2006. Color analysis is provided by former Irish All-American tailback Allen Pinkett—with WNDU-TV sports director Jeff Jeffers adding sideline commentary, along with pregame and halftime commentary.

84 Television Ratings

Notre Dame Sets the Pace

As hard as it may be to believe, college football used to be a relative rarity when it came to television.

There were no midweek games. ESPN did not exist. And the NCAA still controlled broadcast rights until 1984.

That meant the select few games shown on Saturdays drew comparatively high ratings because they had no competition from other games. And those factors combined to create some huge ratings for some of Notre Dame's greatest games.

For example, the top-rated college football games of all-time include Notre Dame–USC in 1968 (22.9 rating, with each rating point representing one percent of all television households in the country), Notre Dame–Michigan State in 1966 (22.5), Notre Dame–USC in 1970 (22.2), Notre Dame–USC in 1974 (20.9) and Notre Dame–USC in 1972 (20.4), all of them on ABC Sports.

After deregulation in 1984, the top regular-season games included Notre Dame–Florida State on NBC in 1993 (16.0), Notre Dame–Miami on CBS in 1989 (14.9), Notre Dame–USC on ABC in 1988 (14.5), Notre Dame–USC on CBS in 1989 (10.9), Notre Dame–Michigan on ABC in 1989 (10.5) and Notre Dame–USC on ABC in 1990 (10.1). The epic Notre Dame–Miami clash in 1988 drew a 9.5 rating on CBS.

Notre Dame's strong bowl run in the late 1980s, '90s, and beyond also earned impressive numbers:

- 15.0 for the 1989 Fiesta Bowl vs. West Virginia on NBC
- 18.5 for the 1990 Orange Bowl vs. Colorado on NBC
- 17.5 for the 1991 Orange Bowl vs. Colorado on NBC
- 11.4 for the 1992 Sugar Bowl vs. Florida on ABC
- 10.2 for the 1993 Cotton Bowl vs. Texas A&M on NBC
- 11.3 for the 1994 Cotton Bowl vs. Texas A&M on NBC
- 6.0 for the 1995 Fiesta Bowl vs. Colorado on NBC
- 12.5 for the 1996 Orange Bowl vs. Florida State on CBS
- 10.7 for the 2001 Fiesta Bowl vs. Oregon State on ABC
- 12.9 for the 2006 Fiesta Bowl vs. Ohio State on ABC
- 9.29 for the 2007 Sugar Bowl vs. LSU on FOX

Notre Dame's win over Pittsburgh in 1990 earned a 6.5, at that time the best ever for an ESPN regular season game. The Notre Dame–Penn State game in 1990 on ESPN also drew a 6.5 rating.

Irish Guard

Stately Escorts for the Band

As the Notre Dame band—the Band of the Fighting Irish—enters Notre Dame Stadium for its pregame salute, it is led by the drum major who is closely followed by the famous Irish Guard. Each member is dressed in an Irish kilt and towers more than eight feet tall with his bearskin shako. The guardsmen are skilled marchers who are chosen for this honor on the basis of marching ability, appearance, and spirit.

The late John Fyfe, originally from Glasgow, Scotland, served as the long-standing adviser to the Irish Guard. The uniform of the Guard is patterned after the traditional Irish kilt.

According to Seumas Uah Urthuile, an Irish historian, laws were introduced in Ireland about 1000 A.D. concerning the use of colors in clothing in order to distinguish between various occupations, military rank, and the various stages of the social and political spectrum.

The Irish Guard's colors are significant to Notre Dame and utilize the Notre Dame plaid. The gold and blue represents the school colors intermixed with green for the Irish. The doublets are papal red.

86 Clashmore Mike

The Original Notre Dame Mascot

The mascot of the Notre Dame football team during the 1930s through the '50s was actually a succession of Irish terrier dogs. The first, named Brick Top Shaun-Rhu, was donated by Cleveland native Charles Otis and was presented to football coach Knute Rockne the week of the 1930 Notre Dame–Pennsylvania game.

There was a companion mascot named Pat in the 1950s, along with several female terriers—but most of Notre Dame's terrier mascots were known as Clashmore Mike. Football game programs

A succession of Irish terrier dogs named Clashmore Mike served as the football team's mascot from the 1930s through the 1950s.

in the 1930s and '40s included a regular "column" from Clashmore Mike, who was also the subject of a 1949 book titled, *Mascot Mike of Notre Dame*. The feisty terrier appeared on the cover of the 1963 Notre Dame Football "Dope Book" alongside head coach Hugh Devore and captain Bob Lehman.

Two years later, the leprechaun—which is consistent with the Notre Dame athletic teams' nickname of the Fighting Irish—was registered as an official University mark, with the leprechaun mascot going on to be a regular part of the game-day atmosphere alongside the Notre Dame cheerleaders.

87 Father Jim Riehle

Irish Chaplain Earned Legend Status

He never played or coached in a single game for Notre Dame, but for decades there was no more familiar figure on the sidelines of Irish athletic events than longtime athletic chaplain Rev. James Riehle, C.S.C.

A long list of current and former Notre Dame athletics coaches and administrators came to pay tribute to the longtime athletic chaplain and Notre Dame Monogram Club executive director following his October 2008 death.

Among the pallbearers were former Notre Dame hockey coach Charles "Lefty" Smith (1968/69–1986/87), Notre Dame assistant athletics director and former assistant football coach Brian Boulac, former Irish football captain and former Monogram Club president Jim Carroll, former Monogram Club president and former Irish football player Mike Heaton, and current Monogram Club executive director Jim Fraleigh.

Following the 2008 death of longtime athletic chaplain Rev. James Riehle, C.S.C., former university president Rev. Theodore M. Hesburgh said, "He was one of the great ones here in a quiet way."

Serving as honorary pallbearers were former Notre Dame football coaches Ara Parseghian (1964–74), Gerry Faust (1981–85), and Lou Holtz (1986–96), current Irish football coach Charlie Weis, former Irish men's basketball coach Richard "Digger" Phelps (1971/72–1990/91), current Notre Dame men's and women's basketball coaches Mike Brey and Muffet McGraw—and former Notre Dame athletics directors Dick Rosenthal (1987–95) and Kevin White (2000–2008).

One of the readers at the funeral Mass was former Monogram Club president Marty Allen. Others in attendance included former University president Rev. Edward Malloy, C.S.C., former Monogram Club president and Irish football captain Jim Lynch, former Monogram Club president and former Irish volleyball player Julie Doyle, former Monogram Club executive director and current senior associate athletics director Bill Scholl, former South Bend mayor and Indiana Governor Joe Kernan (who also played baseball at Notre Dame), current athletics director Jack Swarbrick and 1980 football captain John Scully. Among those attending the visitation was former Notre Dame football coach Bob Davie (1997–2001).

Former Notre Dame president Rev. Theodore M. Hesburgh, C.S.C., spoke at the Mass, describing how he first met Riehle on the second floor of Badin Hall (where Hesburgh lived) when Riehle first returned to Notre Dame as a student after World War II. Hesburgh talked about breaking the news of the death of Riehle's father to him—and how Riehle, as the university's "prefect of discipline," played a major role in maintaining peace among students on campus during the Vietnam war years.

"Jim also was enamored with the wonderful tradition of sports at Notre Dame and he was the greatest friend our athletes had. I can't tell you how many medals of Our Lady he distributed to our athletes before games. There was no question about his love for our students, their competitive nature and their spirit," Hesburgh said.

"He was there when student-athletes needed him—and he was there with firmness and with love, as a friend and as a mentor. He was one of the great ones here in a quiet way."

Presiding at the Mass was Rev. Anthony V. Szakaly, C.S.C., Assistant Provincial of the Indiana Province of the Congregation of Holy Cross.

Riehle served as Monogram Club executive director from 1978 through 2002, then he continued to work with the club in an emeritus role. He began as the chaplain for the athletic department in 1966, officially earning the title in 1973. His first football game as Notre Dame team chaplain was the famous 10–10 tie with Michigan State in 1966.

"Father was a true Notre Dame man who dedicated his life to his faith and to the university," Fraleigh said. "He touched the lives of thousands of Notre Dame students and student-athletes—and he was the driving force behind the initiatives of the Monogram Club."

A 1949 graduate of Notre Dame, Riehle earned his bachelor's degree in business administration and then studied theology at Holy Cross College in Washington, D.C., from 1960–64. He earned his master's degree in business administration from Notre Dame in 1978.

Riehle was ordained as a deacon at the Shrine of the Immaculate Conception in Washington, D.C., in 1963. On June 10, 1964, he was ordained as a priest in Notre Dame's Sacred Heart Church. His first assignment was as chaplain for Dillon Hall before he went to Sacred Heart Parish in New Orleans, Louisiana. In 1966, Riehle returned to Notre Dame as the assistant dean of students and rector of Sorin Hall. He assumed the dean of students post in 1967 and served in that capacity until 1973. For 12 years, until 1985, Riehle served as rector of Pangborn Hall.

Born November 25, 1924, and originally from Saginaw, Michigan, Riehle held several posts at the university, including chairman of the board of directors for the University Club (1971–77) and director of energy conservation (1973–93).

In recognition of his contributions to the athletic department and the University of Notre Dame, he was honored with the 2001 Moose Krause Man of the Year Award by the Monogram Club, and the intramural fields located on the north end of the campus (just east of Stepan Center) were named in his honor.

The Monogram Club fund that assists former Irish athletes with funding for their children to attend Notre Dame is named the Brennan-Boland-Riehle Scholarship Fund in his honor.

Formerly an enthusiastic hockey player and long an avid cigar-smoker and golfer, Riehle played the role of Notre Dame football team chaplain in the movie *Rudy*. He also starred in an Adidas commercial in which he facetiously asked former Irish quarterback Joe Montana, "What have you been doing since you left the university?"

88 The Shirt

A Fundraising Tradition Season after Season

The Shirt Project began at Notre Dame in 1990 through the vision and leadership of Brennan Harvath, a 1991 Notre Dame graduate.

As chairman of the Student Union Board's AnTostal spring celebration, Harvath envisioned raising money to supplement the AnTostal budget by selling a T-shirt to Notre Dame students.

"The Shirt," as it became known, was intended to unify the student section in the football stadium for the home opener against Michigan on September 15, 1990. With Notre Dame and Michigan having similar team colors, Harvath's vision was for the crowd to be unified in green, symbolic of the Fighting Irish. More than 9,000 Shirts were sold, and more than 85 percent of the student body wore The Shirt to the game.

More than $17,000 was raised to create new AnTostal events, and a portion of the funds was also allocated to each residence hall. Due to the popularity of The Shirt 1990, the program continued the following year with the Student Union Board AnTostal Chairman once again coordinating the project. As the success and notoriety of The Shirt continued to grow, revenue exceeded the needs of the Student Union Board. The Shirt Project became its own student organization, and student leaders decided to distribute the profits to other student organizations.

In 1993, profits were dedicated to offset the medical expenses of a student who was paralyzed, and additional funds that year were used to establish memorial scholarships in the names of Meghan Beeler and Colleen Hipp, members of the Notre Dame varsity swimming team who were killed in a bus accident in 1992.

To this day, money raised through sales of The Shirt continues to be allocated to Notre Dame residence halls and student organizations, as well as to create memorial scholarships in the names of Notre Dame students.

Fifty percent of proceeds are contributed to The Shirt Charity Fund, which supports Notre Dame students who suffer catastrophic illnesses and accidents. The Rector Fund, which makes funding available for students to take part in unique Notre Dame experiences (service learning trips, football tickets, club activities, residence hall events, and other quality-of-life activities), also receives a portion of the revenue.

The Shirt 2006 was the most successful to date, with more than 155,000 sold and $650,000 in net profits.

The success of the Student Union Board's green-shirt campaign for the 1990 Michigan game was recognized by Sister Jean Lenz, who at the time was serving as assistant vice president in the Office of Student Affairs. Sister Jean was providing support for Zhengde Wang, a Chinese doctoral student with plans to enroll in the Notre Dame Law School, who was seriously injured when he was hit by a car in November 1989.

As Wang's medical expenses increased, Lenz approached Joe Cassidy, director of student activities, with the idea of creating another shirt with the proceeds intended to help Wang and his family, who moved to South Bend to stay with him during his recovery. With the October 20, 1990, game against Miami drawing near, Cassidy and Lenz presented the idea to the Hall Presidents

Council, and student leaders agreed to support the fundraiser by selling the shirts on campus.

Media attention was generated through the support of the athletics department, and all 17,000 navy blue shirts printed for the game were sold out before kickoff. A second version of the shirt was printed after the game bearing the Notre Dame winning 29–20 score, and an additional 15,300 of these were sold. The 32,300 total shirts sold resulted in a $100,000 check being presented to Wang and his family to cover their expenses.

89 Fighting Irish Cover Boys

Gracing *Sports Illustrated*

Notre Dame football is no stranger to the cover of *Sports Illustrated*.

The Irish have been featured on the cover of the magazine 34 times, with the most recent being when Irish captains Brady Quinn, Travis Thomas, and Tom Zbikowski appeared on the cover of the 2006 college football preview edition (one of a half-dozen regional covers).

Notre Dame was also featured on *Sports Illustrated* covers during back-to-back weeks in November 1993. After the Irish knocked off top-ranked Florida State in '93, the November 22 cover featured Jim Flanigan and the headline "We Did It." One week later, Notre Dame lost to Boston College on a last-second field goal, and that week's cover showed Eagle players celebrating and the headline "Down Goes No. 1 Again."

Notre Dame was also featured on the *SI* cover three times during the 1988 national championship season, including a cover that showed Tony Rice leading the win over West Virginia in the Fiesta Bowl.

The first Notre Dame player to grace the cover of the magazine was quarterback Paul Hornung on October 29, 1956, previewing the Oklahoma game.

Other Notre Dame cover appearances include: October 26, 1959—George Izo; November 2, 1964—John Huarte; November 7, 1966—Terry Hanratty; November 28, 1966—overall shot of 10–10 tie with Michigan State; September 11, 1967—Hanratty; October 9, 1967—Irish defense in win over Purdue; November 9, 1970—Joe Theismann; January 11, 1971—Theismann; November 5, 1973—action shot of Notre Dame win over USC; September 30, 1974—Tom Clements; December 9, 1974—Notre Dame defense in loss to USC; September 29, 1975—Rick Slager and coach Dan Devine; September 5, 1977—Ross Browner; January 9, 1978—Terry Eurick; September 24, 1979—Vagas Ferguson; November 5, 1984—Gerry Faust; September 22, 1986—overall shot of Michigan win over Notre Dame; August 31, 1987—Tim Brown; October 24, 1988—Tony Rice; December 5, 1988—Rice; January 9, 1989—Rice; September 4, 1989—Lou Holtz; September 25, 1989—Raghib Ismail; November 27, 1989—Rice; December 4, 1989—Ned Bolcar; September 24, 1990—Rick Mirer; November 26, 1990—overall shot of Notre Dame vs. Penn State game; September 23, 1996—Ron Powlus; September 23, 2002—Maurice Stovall vs. Michigan State.

A montage of Irish football images was part of the cover of the *Sports Illustrated Presents Notre Dame* commemorative issue published in October 2006.

The Notre Dame leader for overall career *Sports Illustrated* covers is Joe Montana, who was pictured on 13 covers.

90 Bookstore Basketball

No Shortage of Gridiron Talent on Hardcourt

Bookstore Basketball bills itself as the "largest outdoor 5-on–5 tournament in the world." In 2008, 694 teams of students and other individuals associated with the university competed in this single-elimination event played under iron-man rules (that means games are played no matter the weather and no matter who is hurt on your roster).

A good-natured competitor, coach Lou Holtz, shown here defending Tim Brown, plays to win—even on the basketball court.

Yet even a basketball event at Notre Dame maintains its share of football overtones. In fact, Irish quarterbacks in particular have enjoyed their share of success in the event that began in 1972 and was featured by *Sports Illustrated* in 1978 (when writer Rick Telander came to South Bend and played on a team).

Irish All-American hoop star John Shumate became the MVP of that initial tournament in '72. But among his successors have been Notre Dame football names like Tom Clements ('75), Rusty Lisch ('80), Tony Hunter and Greg Williamson ('82), Eric Jones ('94), Mike Denvir ('97), Justin Tuck ('02), Chinedum Ndukwe ('06), and Robbie Parris ('07).

Clements played on two teams that won Bookstore titles. Joe Montana claimed one crown, and Lisch won three straight from 1978–80. Steve Beuerlein carried on the tradition, Tony Rice twice came in as runner-up, Brady Quinn won a title, and Dayne Crist in 2009 became the most recent quarterback to claim a blue ribbon. Former Irish defensive back John Dubenetzky also played on three straight winning teams from 1975–77.

Irish football coaches like Gerry Faust and Lou Holtz made on-court appearances—and Bookstore commissioners routinely select an all-(last name of current head football coach) team at the end of the event based on the top varsity footballers to take part.

91 Walk the LaBar Practice Complex Fields

Home to Irish Practices

The LaBar Practice Complex, Notre Dame's new three-field football practice facility, was dedicated on the morning of Notre Dame's 2008 season-opening football game against San Diego State.

The three fields, two of them artificial turf, are adjacent to the Guglielmino Athletics Complex and comprise a $2.5 million project that was based on the benefaction of John R. "Rees" LaBar, a 1953 Notre Dame graduate, and his wife, Carol, who reside in Cincinnati, Ohio, and in Long Boat Key, Florida.

The LaBars have a grandson, David, who was a 2008 Notre Dame graduate, and a granddaughter, Lindsay, who was a junior at Notre Dame in 2008–09.

Rees and Carol LaBar together are two of the largest contributors in Notre Dame history to undergraduate scholarships for deserving students. More than 100 students from the Cincinnati area have attended Notre Dame as a result of their long-time financial support. In addition, the LaBars have endowed the directorship for Academic Services for Student-Athletes, the department that provides academic support for Notre Dame's 650 student-athletes. They have also created two Hesburgh Library endowments.

A groundbreaking ceremony was held in October 2007 on the morning of the Notre Dame–USC football game to signify the start of the project. The project was completed in time for the early August start of Notre Dame's 2008 fall football camp.

The FieldTurf practice fields are available for use primarily by the football squad, but also for lacrosse, soccer, and RecSports use. The fields are located side by side at the far north end of the former Cartier Field configuration. They help meet the year-round demand for high-quality practice fields and also reduce demand for the Loftus Center indoor field. Each field is lighted and secured by an 8-foot fence, with an adjacent maintenance building to provide storage.

The former track, grass field, and bleachers within Moose Krause Stadium were removed beginning in April 2008, making room for the three new fields. A new track then was constructed just north of Edison Road, adjacent to (and east of) Leahy Drive, and southwest of Eck Baseball Stadium.

The construction of the new football fields was one of the dominos in the series of recent facility additions and changes that also include construction of new stadia for lacrosse, soccer, track and field, and tennis, all within the large area east of the Joyce Center. All these projects were part of the university's "Spirit of Notre Dame" campaign.

92 Bengal Bouts

Browner-MacAfee a Beauty in 1976

The Bengal Bouts have a long and colorful history on the Notre Dame campus as the University boxing club's annual championships benefiting the Holy Cross missions in Bangladesh. In fact, football coach Knute Rockne actually started the bouts in 1920 as a method to keep his football players in shape in the off-season.

Football coaches eventually decided the Bengals maybe shouldn't be the priority they once represented, and that's been a loss for the Bengals because Irish gridders earned their share of headlines and applause.

Those who were there to witness it still talk about the 1976 Joyce Center super-heavyweight confrontation between defensive end Ross Browner and tight end Ken MacAfee. It was a heavyweight fight in every sense of the word. The two football All-Americans traded punches from the opening bell to the final seconds before Browner won by a split decision.

Linebacker Doug Becker beat safety Jim Browner for the heavyweight title that same night—as the four Irish football stars thrilled a crowd of nearly 10,000 spectators that night at the Joyce Center.

For a number of years, NBC Sports televised the Bengal Bouts finals from the Joyce Center, taping the bouts and combining them with Irish hurling as part of a St. Patrick's Day show that aired on a Saturday afternoon edition of NBC's anthology *SportsWorld*.

93 Take a Tour

A Gastronomic View of South Bend/Notre Dame

Cities like South Bend often earn a bad rap when it comes to food. Okay, so we understand this isn't the upper east side of Manhattan where you can find all kinds of tony Italian eateries and one-of-a-kind delis that offer all the gastronomic delights you could ever hope to sample. But South Bend isn't the foodie wasteland some would make it out to be.

We'll give you some hints where you should stop, some of them well known and others a bit off the beaten track. Either way, they offer noteworthy alternatives to the chain options you can find most anywhere.

Fine dining? Try the LaSalle Grill downtown or the Carriage House, a genteel option out in the country way west of town. There's also Yesterday's in downtown Granger (huge portions and awesome homemade deserts) and the Main Street Grill in downtown Mishawaka (not very big and not as well known, but an excellent spot).

Want Italian? Try Carmela's (near downtown on Niles Avenue) or Villa Macri (in Granger), both part of a longtime South Bend family connection.

A sucker for sweets? You can't beat the South Bend Chocolate Company. It became so popular there are now locations all over the state, including on the Indiana Toll Road. Ever been to the Cherry Republic, a celebration of everything cherry in the burg of Glen Arbor, Michigan? The Cherry Republic sends its locally grown cherries all the way to South Bend to have them chocolatized. That's all you need to know. My father loves the chocolate-covered peanuts so much he has me send him regular care packages of them. There's also yummy caramel corn laced seasonally with various items depending on whether it's Christmas, St. Patrick's Day or Valentine's Day.

Wandering the campus on Saturday? Try a steak sandwich at the Knights of Columbus hall on the South Quad. It's a step up from the usual dogs or brats.

Thirsty for an adult beverage? You've got to make at least one stop at the Linebacker at Edison and Rt. 23. It's been there forever, and the old-school sign out front says it all. Any place that refers to itself as a lounge is obviously secure in its image. The Linebacker has re-invented itself a number of times (amazingly, it was better known for its noon-hour lingerie shows not that many years ago). But at its best, it's a college bar, especially since the original Five Points haunts like Corby's, Nicky's, Goose's, and the Library are long since gone.

A more gentrified option is Legends, just south of Notre Dame Stadium. On the site of the former Senior Bar (it still shares space with a student dance club), Legends' calling is the two-dozen beer varieties it has on tap.

Looking for a breakfast option? Try Studebagel's on Rt. 23 just east of campus. They've got homemade bagels, and they're also open through lunch with sandwich options. Former Irish basketball player and current deputy athletics director Missy Conboy originally opened Studebagel's.

94 Books on Parade

No Shortage of Tomes on the Irish

You can easily fill a bookshelf with books written about Notre Dame football and all its moving pieces. I've got dozens in my office and another selection at home.

It's amazing how many were written about Knute Rockne immediately following his death in 1931.

One of the more interesting items in my collection is a 6" x 9", 64-page, soft-cover edition titled *Knute Rockne's Career*. Loaded with photos, it's somewhere between a magazine and a paperback. Published in 1931 by Modern Magazines Inc. out of Minneapolis, Minnesota, it sold for 50 cents. I picked it up at a garage sale (as a kid in South Bend) for a dollar.

With all due respect to the various authors and publishers who have written about Irish football, here are a handful of recommendations of interesting options—some a little off the beaten track. Many of these are technically out of print, but the secondary market through Web sites like Amazon, Barnes & Noble, and Borders (among others) makes it much easier to track them down (listed in order of publication):

Notre Dame Football: The T Formation by Frank Leahy (Prentice-Hall, 1949)—Want to know exactly how the Irish offense was designed to work? You can't do any better than reading it in the words of the man who made the T-formation work, Hall of Fame coach Frank Leahy. Dedicated to the memory of Knute Rockne, the copy I have came from the book's fourth printing. It would be interesting to know how many of these books still sit on the office shelves of current major-college head coaches.

The Glory of Notre Dame edited by Fred Katz (Bartholomew House, 1971)—*SPORT* magazine began publishing in 1946 and has been defunct since 2000, but this is a collection of 22 essays reprinted from its pages. With stories that spanned the decades from Rockne to Parseghian, its authors include literary sports legends like Grantland Rice, Jimmy Breslin, Dick Schaap, and Roger Kahn.

Parseghian and Notre Dame Football by Ara Parseghian and Tom Pagna (Men-in-Motion, 1971)—Ara and his offensive coordinator Pagna combine to explain every last nuance of how they ran the Notre Dame program—with lots of Xs and Os and other diagrams.

Shake Down the Thunder by Wells Twombly (Chilton, 1974)—This was billed as the "official" Frank Leahy biography and was published a year after Leahy's 1973 death. Written by esteemed *San Francisco Examiner* columnist Wells Twombly (he himself died in 1977 at age 41), it's a no-holds-barred look at Leahy and everything that happened to him and his family on and off the field. The dedication suggests Leahy "may have been America's last knight-errant."

Wake Up The Echoes—Notre Dame Football by Ken Rappoport (Strode Publishers, 1975)—Strode Publishers out of Huntsville, Alabama, produced more than two dozen histories of college football programs back in the 1970s. All of these are generally well done and serve as great archival pieces—and Rappoport, who also did the USC and Penn State versions, did the Notre Dame edition. This book still might serve as the most comprehensive history of Irish football on the shelves.

Notre Dame's Era of Ara by Tom Pagna with Bob Best (Strode Publishers, 1976)—After Parseghian's retirement, Pagna and assistant Notre Dame publicist Best put together this anecdote-laden, season-by-season look at the Parseghian years. Now available in paperback, it remains the most in-depth look at everything that happened while Ara was at Notre Dame.

Out of Bounds: An Anecdotal History of Notre Dame Football by Michael Bonifer and L.G. Weaver (Piper Publishing, 1978)—This is a rather quirky piece by a couple of guys with no particular ties to Notre Dame and no extensive writing resumes. But it's a very light and fun take on Irish football, with lots of material you won't find other places.

Before Rockne at Notre Dame by Chet Grant (Icarus Press, 1978)—Not so long ago, when someone wanted to talk about Knute Rockne and old-time Notre Dame football, the people we sent them to were Moose Krause and Chet Grant. Fortunately, Grant (who played quarterback for the Irish during Rockne's time) put his recollections into book form, and this piece provides a nice look at how football worked at Notre Dame before Rockne arrived.

Knute Rockne: A Bio-Bibliography by Michael R. Steele (Greenwood Press, 1983)—There are dozens of books on Rockne. This one is more of a scholarly effort by a Pacific University English professor (Steele is also responsible for *The Fighting Irish Football Encyclopedia*). It's well-researched and comes at you from different angles than most of the treatments of the former Irish coach— including excellent interview transcriptions.

The Fighting Spirit: A Championship Season at Notre Dame by Lou Holtz (Pocket Books, 1989)—This was Holtz's first-person story of what turned out to be a national championship season in 1988 (in the interest of full disclosure, I assisted with this project). I convinced Holtz that, for all the things that had been written about Notre Dame, no one had ever done a book detailing exactly what happens from one day to the next for a full year and why the job is so challenging. The fact that Notre Dame won the title proved to be icing on the cake. Holtz didn't leave anything to the imagination.

The Biggest Game of Them All: Notre Dame, Michigan State and the Fall of '66 by Mike Celizic (Simon & Schuster, 1992)—This is much more than a treatise on one legendary football game. Celizic, later a columnist for *The Record* in Bergen County, New Jersey (and now an MSNBC.com contributor), was a freshman student at Notre Dame in 1966. He lived the event and after the fact did a superb job of interviewing and researching the participants. This book captures the time and place of college football at its highest level in the '60s. One recent college football history book rated it one of the top 10 books on college football of the last 50 years.

The Fighting Irish on the Air by Paul F. Gullifor (Diamond Communications, 2001)—This effort didn't necessarily become a *New York Times* bestseller—but for the hard-core Irish fan, it's a great look at the history and details of Notre Dame's electronic media exposure through the years. It's easily the most detailed analysis of all the hows and whys of the Notre Dame–NBC Sports relationship. Gullifor is a South Bend native who became a professor at Bradley University.

Echoes of Notre Dame Football: Great and Memorable Moments of the Fighting Irish by Joe Garner (Sourcebooks MediaFusion, 2001)—Garner made his name with a series of books that featured great collections of historic audio and video, including bestsellers *And the Crowd Goes Wild, And the Fans Roared,* and *We Interrupt This Broadcast.* This time Garner jumped into the sports realm and the most noteworthy aspect is what's comprised on the two audio CDs as narrated by Regis Philbin.

Shake Down the Thunder: The Creation of Notre Dame Football by Murray A. Sperber (Indiana University Press, 2002)—Sperber is best known for his jousting with Bob Knight when Sperber was an English and American Studies professor at Indiana University. He also became a cultural expert on college football based on this book and several others he did (*College Sports, Inc.; Onward to Victory:*

The Crises that Shaped College Sports; and *Beer and Circus*). He made great use of Rockne's collection of papers and correspondence in the Notre Dame archives and did a superb job of explaining how football at Notre Dame and all over the country fit into the cultural backdrop of the times. Maybe the most interesting thing you learn is that in Rockne's time, he hired the on-field officials for Notre Dame games—and they were the same people who worked for newspapers covering the games. Sperber is now a visiting professor at the University of California–Berkeley.

95 College All-Star Game

A Long-Lost Tradition

Longtime *Chicago Tribune* sportswriter Arch Ward (in addition to originating the Major League Baseball All-Star Game) began the College All-Star Game, a midsummer football game between the defending National Football League champions and a team of college players who had used up their eligibility.

Born in Irwin, Illinois, Ward first attended Loras College, moved on to St. Joseph's College (both in Dubuque, Iowa), then finished at Notre Dame where he also worked as a publicist for Knute Rockne. So Ward was hardly a stranger to football in South Bend.

He became sports editor of the *Tribune* in 1930 and remained in that role until his death in 1955. He started the baseball event in 1933, then he followed up with the college All-Star idea a year later. He also started the All-American Football Conference, a new pro league, in 1946.

In its heyday, the College All-Star game qualified as one of the sports highlights of the summer. Here are Irish players who started in the College All-Star contest over the years:

1934   T Moose Krause (he recovered a fumble inside his own 20 in the second period to help preserve a 0–0 tie with the Chicago Bears)

1936   E Wayne Millner
        HB Bill Shakespeare

1938   E Chuck Sweeney
        QB Andy Puplis

1939   E Earl Brown
        Coach Elmer Layden

1940   T Tad Harvey
        FB Joe Thesing

1942   G Bernie Crimmins

1943   E Bill Huber

1944   E John Yonakor
        FB Creighton Miller (his first-period touchdown reception from Tulsa's Glenn Dobbs helped the All-Stars to an early 14–0 leading before they lost 24–21 to the Chicago Bears)

1945   E Bill Huber

1947   T Joe Mastrangelo
        QB George Ratterman (the All-Stars defeated the Chicago Bears 17–0, as Ratterman threw a 46-yard touchdown strike to Notre Dame's Jack Zilly)
        FB Jim Mello (he added a six-yard, first-period scoring run)
        Coach Frank Leahy

1948   T George Connor
        T Ziggy Czarobski
        QB Johnny Lujack
        Coach Frank Leahy

1949   G Marty Wendell
       G Bill Fischer
1950   E Jim Martin
1951   C Jerry Groom
       QB Bob Williams
1954   G Menil Mavraides
       HB Johnny Lattner (the All-Stars' only points in a 31–6 loss to the Detroit Lions came on a Lattner four-yard, third-period touchdown run)
       FB Neil Worden
1955   T Frank Varrichione
       C Dick Szymanski
       QB Ralph Guglielmi (he threw a touchdown pass to Henry Hair in the 30–27 win over the Cleveland Browns, with former Irish star George Ratterman throwing for one score and running for another for the Browns)
1956   FB Don Schaefer (Ratterman threw another touchdown pass in the Cleveland Browns' 26–0 win)
1959   FB Nick Pietrosante (former Notre Dame standout Jim Mutscheller caught a touchdown pass from Johnny Unitas in the Baltimore Colts' 29–0 victory)
1960   QB George Izo
1962   OT Joe Carollo
       DB Angelo Dabiero
1964   DT George Bednar
1965   (Notre Dame's John Huarte didn't start—Navy's Roger Staubach did—but Huarte threw two second-half scoring passes in the 24–16 Cleveland Browns' win)
1966   DB Nick Rassas
1967   OG Tom Regner
       DE Alan Page
       LB Jim Lynch
1968   LB Mike McGill

1969   E Jim Seymour
        OT George Kunz
        QB Terry Hanratty
1970   DT Mike McCoy
1972   DE Walt Patulski
1975   DE Mike Fanning (former Irish back Rocky Bleier caught
        a touchdown pass from the Steelers' Joe Gilliam in a 21–14
        Pittsburgh win)
1976   Coach Ara Parseghian

The game ended after the 1976 event. In all but two seasons, the game was played at Soldier Field in Chicago—and proceeds went to Chicago Tribune Charities Inc., which distributed millions of dollars to various organizations.

Opening Day

The 1887 Michigan Game

The names of the players are not memorable for any particular reason.

In fact, there's no record of who actually scored in the University of Notre Dame's first official football game against the University of Michigan in 1887.

The Wolverines won the game 8–0, the first of eight straight series wins by Michigan (Notre Dame wouldn't beat the Wolverines until 1909).

The Michigan team was treated to lunch, then the team took off for Chicago for another game. The event was a far cry from what Notre Dame football is about today. In fact, as much as anything, this game involved the Notre Dame students learning the game of football, which at the time was a fairly new phenomenon.

In any event, it's suggested that there was some amount of passion around campus involving this first-time contest—and that probably shouldn't come as any surprise given what we know about Notre Dame football today.

97 ESPN's *College GameDay*

Come to South Bend When It's on Campus

The creation of the Saturday morning *College GameDay* show by ESPN has arguably done as much as anything to promote the game of college football.

The show began in the studio in Bristol, Connecticut, back in 1987. Lee Corso has been with the show since its inception, Chris Fowler joined the crew in 1990, Kirk Herbstreit came on board in 1996, and Desmond Howard most recently in 2005. Former Irish All-Star Raghib Ismail was part of the show during the 2003 and '04 seasons.

GameDay first went on the road for the 1993 Notre Dame–Florida State No. 1 vs. No. 2 battle from Notre Dame Stadium. Mostly because of weather concerns for that November 13 matchup, the indoor site for the show was the second-floor concourse of the Joyce Center.

More recent early-season matchups have prompted the show to select an outdoor location on the Notre Dame Hesburgh Library mall, just north of Notre Dame Stadium.

Notre Dame has been part of the *GameDay* festivities on 18 occasions, including seven stops in South Bend (including five in a row to start the series, among those 18).

Notre Dame has welcomed ESPN to South Bend on seven occasions as the broadcast site of the network's College GameDay *show. The Irish have been part of 18 matchups featured on the popular Saturday morning show.*

Here's a complete listing of Irish games at which *GameDay* has appeared (Irish are 8–10 overall with *GameDay* present, including 3–4 at Notre Dame Stadium):

- 1993—No. 1 Florida State at No. 2 Notre Dame (Notre Dame won 31–24, to move to No. 1, in what is arguably the most hyped game in Notre Dame Stadium history)

- 1994—No. 6 Michigan at No. 3 Notre Dame (Michigan won 26–24, on a Remy Hamilton field goal with two seconds left)
- 1995—No. 5 USC at No. 17 Notre Dame (the Irish prevailed 38–10 by converting 15 of 20 third downs)
- 1996—No. 4 Ohio State at No. 5 Notre Dame (the Buckeyes won, 29–16, behind Pepe Pearson's 173 rushing yards)
- 1998—No. 5 Michigan at No. 22 Notre Dame (the Irish defeated the defending national champions and Tom Brady 36–20—after trailing 13–6 at half—with Autry Denson gaining 162 yards)
- 1999—No. 16 Notre Dame at No. 7 Michigan (the Irish fell 26–22)
- 1999—No. 24 Notre Dame at No. 4 Tennessee (Vols won 38–14)
- 2000—No. 1 Nebraska at No. 23 Notre Dame (Huskers needed OT to win 27–24)
- 2001—No. 23 Notre Dame at No. 5 Nebraska (Huskers prevailed again, 27–10)
- 2002—No. 7 Notre Dame at No. 18 Air Force (Irish won, 21–14, outrushing the Falcons 335–104)
- 2002—No. 6 Notre Dame at No. 11 Florida State (Irish won, 34–24, in the high point of the Tyrone Willingham era, in Notre Dame's only-ever trip to Tallahassee)
- 2003—Notre Dame at No. 5 Michigan (Wolverines won 38–0)
- 2004—Notre Dame at Michigan State (Irish won 31–24, forcing six turnovers)
- 2004—Notre Dame at No. 1 USC (Trojans prevailed 41–10)
- 2005—Notre Dame at No. 23 Pittsburgh (Notre Dame won 42–21 in the first game of the Charlie Weis era)

- 2005—No. 1 USC at No. 9 Notre Dame (Trojans survived 34–31 on Matt Leinart's controversial late touchdown)
- 2006—No. 2 Notre Dame at Georgia Tech (Irish won 14–10 against Tech defense coordinated by current Irish assistant Jon Tenuta)
- 2006—No. 6 Notre Dame at No. 3 USC (Trojans won 44–24)

GameDay made its first trip to Notre Dame for men's basketball when the Irish played host to No. 3 Connecticut in January 2009 in a game in which the Irish risked their record 45-game overall home court win streak and their Big East record-tying 20-game home win streak against league opponents.

98 Top 20 Moments in Notre Dame History

The Actual Vote Totals

Notre Dame's 1988 football team claimed a unanimous No. 1 ranking following that season, thanks to a 12–0 record and a victory over third-rated West Virginia in the Fiesta Bowl.

Eleven years later, that same Irish team earned yet another No. 1 finish. Notre Dame's 31–30 triumph over top-rated Miami in 1988 was voted the greatest moment in the last century of Irish football as part of the Century of Greatness program that ran throughout the 1999 Notre Dame season.

So if you don't like our list, the following list was voted on by Irish fans.

That midseason victory in 1988 over the 'Canes ended up atop the list—and was followed, in order, by the Irish comeback to

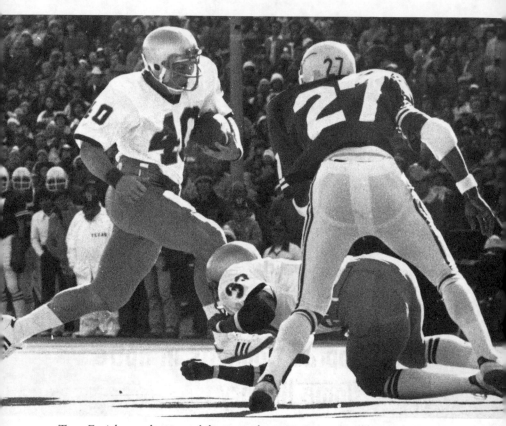

Terry Eurick scored two touchdowns in the 1978 Cotton Bowl as Notre Dame defeated No. 1 Texas, 38–10, to win the game and take over the No. 1 ranking—and that's only No. 16 on the list of the top 20 moments in Notre Dame football history!

defeat Houston in the 1979 Cotton Bowl (second); Notre Dame's 1993 win against top-rated Florida State (third); the Irish win over Army in 1928 in the "Win One for the Gipper" game (fourth); and Notre Dame's 1977 win over USC, which featured a switch to green jerseys (fifth).

The vote totals resulted from balloting at area Meijer stores and on Notre Dame's athletic Web site (www.und.com) throughout August—and from ballots distributed at Notre Dame's 1999 season-opening football game against Kansas.

The Century of Greatness program was a joint promotional effort of the University of Notre Dame, Host Communications, and University Netcasting, with Meijer and Coca-Cola as the title sponsors. Coca-Cola distributed a series of trading cards throughout the season in 12-packs sold at area Meijer stores.

The top 20 moments were featured in a special 24-page insert in the 1999 Notre Dame–Boston College game program. In addition, there were special halftime ceremonies at that game recognizing the final vote totals. Also, Host Communications produced a 45-minute video highlighting the top 20 moments.

The final rankings of the top 20 moments go like this:

1. 1988—Notre Dame defeats top-ranked Miami, 31–30
2. 1979—Montana throws touchdown as time expires in Cotton Bowl win over Houston
3. 1993—Irish defeat top-rated Florida State, 31–24
4. 1928—Notre Dame defeats Army, 12–6, behind Rockne's "Gipper" speech
5. 1977—Irish don green jerseys, defeat fifth-rated USC, 49–19
6. 1935—Notre Dame knocks off Ohio State in Game of the Century
7. 1989—Raghib Ismail returns two kickoffs for touchdowns as Irish beat No. 2 Michigan
8. 1924—Grantland Rice christens Four Horsemen after 13–7 win over Army
9. 1966—Irish and Michigan State end epic matchup in 10–10 tie
10. 1973—Notre Dame prevails, 24–23, in Sugar Bowl game against No. 1 Alabama
11. 1957—Notre Dame's 7–0 win ends Oklahoma's record 47-game win streak
12. 1987—Tim Brown returns two punts for touchdowns as Irish beat Michigan State

13. 1992—Mirer throws for two-point conversion to beat Penn State in the snow
14. 1913—Rockne and Dorais popularize forward pass in 35–13 Irish win at Army
15. 1946—Notre Dame and Army battle to 0–0 tie at Yankee Stadium
16. 1978—Irish knock off top-rated Texas in Cotton Bowl to claim No. 1 spot
17. 1989—Defeat of No. 3 West Virginia 34–21 in Fiesta Bowl to clinch national title
18. 1975—Notre Dame holds off No. 1 Alabama in Orange Bowl in Ara's last game
19. 1980—Oliver's 51-yard field goal as time expires to beat Michigan
20. 1992—Bettis' second-half runs enable Irish to beat Florida in Sugar Bowl

99 The Near Misses

Almost Consensus Irish Titles

Notre Dame routinely considers 11 different seasons in which the Irish claim national championships in football on a consensus basis. These days, that means winning a majority of the titles awarded by the BCS (Bowl Championship Series), Associated Press, Football Writers Association of America (FWAA), National Football Foundation (Grantland Rice Trophy), and *USA Today*/ESPN (the coaches' poll).

But there have been plenty of other seasons where the Irish barely missed out—and in some cases still received some championship mention from the various selectors.

In 119 seasons of football beginning in 1887, Notre Dame has had 101 winning years, only 13 seasons with a losing record (1887, '88, 1933, '56, '60, '63, '81, '85, '86, '99, 2001, '03, and '07) and only five others with a .500 mark (1950, '59, '61, '62, and 2004).

The Fighting Irish have had 12 unbeaten and untied seasons, 10 others in which they were unbeaten but suffered one or more ties, and 28 seasons in which only a single loss spoiled an unbeaten record.

Here is a compilation of Notre Dame's best seasons in its football history:

Unbeaten, Untied

Year	Record	Coach
1889	1–0	None
1912	7–0	John L. Marks
1913	7–0	Jesse Harper
1919	9–0	Knute Rockne
1920	9–0	Knute Rockne
*1924	10–0	Knute Rockne
*1929	9–0	Knute Rockne
*1930	10–0	Knute Rockne
*1947	9–0	Frank Leahy

Irish led final AP poll, but Michigan finished atop most other rankings.

| *1949 | 10–0 | Frank Leahy |

Michigan led first poll, then Irish led final eight.

| *1973 | 11–0 | Ara Parseghian |

Sugar Bowl win over No. 1 Alabama put Irish in top spot for only time all season.

| *1988 | 12–0 | Lou Holtz |

Irish became No. 1 first week of November and held on.

Unbeaten, One or Two Ties

Year	Record	Tie(s)
1892	1–0–1	Hillsdale (10–10)
1903	8–0–1	Northwestern (0–0)
1907	6–0–1	Indiana (0–0)
1909	7–0–1	Marquette (0–0)
1911	6–0–2	Pittsburgh (0–0)
		Marquette (0–0)
1941	8–0–1	Army (0–0)

Irish finished third in final poll, behind Minnesota and Duke.

*1946	8–0–1	Army (0–0)

Irish led only final regular-season poll.

1948	9–0–1	USC (14–14)

The Irish finished second in the final poll to unbeaten Michigan.

1953	9–0–1	Iowa (14–14)

Irish finished as runner-up to Minnesota in final poll.

*1966	9–0–1	Michigan State (10–10)

Irish took over top spot for good once they reached 4–0.

One Loss

Year	Record	Loss
1887	0–1	Michigan (8–0)
1893	4–1	Chicago (8–0)
1894	3–1–1	Albion (19–12)
1895	3–1	Indiana Artillary (18–0)
1897	4–1–1	Chicago (34–5)
1901	8–1–1	Northwestern (2–0)
1906	6–1	Indiana (12–0)
1908	8–1	Michigan (12–6)
1910	4–1–1	Michigan State (17–0)
1915	7–1	Nebraska (20–19)
1916	8–1	Army (30–10)

1917	6–1–1	Nebraska (7–0)
1918	3–1–2	Michigan State (13–7)
1921	10–1	Iowa (10–7)
1922	8–1–1	Nebraska (14–6)
1923	9–1	Nebraska (14–7)
1926	9–1	Carnegie Tech (19–0)
1927	7–1–1	Army (18–0)
1935	7–1–1	Northwestern (14–7)
1938	8–1	USC (13–0)

Irish were fifth in final poll, after leading for three weeks in November.

*1943	9–1	Great Lakes (19–14)

Irish spent entire season ranked atop poll, the only time in history that has happened.

1954	9–1	Purdue (27–14)

Irish led after first win, then were fourth in final poll.

1964	9–1	USC (20–17)

The Irish were 73 seconds away from a consensus title when the Trojans came back from a 17–0 halftime deficit to take the lead.

1970	10–1	USC (38–28)

Irish ended up No. 2 in final poll after Cotton Bowl win over No. 1 Texas.

*1977	11–1	Mississippi (20–13)

Cotton Bowl win over No. 1 Texas vaulted Irish to top spot only in final poll.

1989	12–1	Miami (27–10)

The Irish defended their national title in impressive fashion, winning a school-record 23 straight games before falling to the Hurricanes in the regular-season finale.

1992	10–1–1	Stanford (33–16)

Irish trailed only Alabama, Florida State, and Miami in final poll.

1993	11–1	Boston College (41–39)

The Irish had defeated unbeaten and top-rated Florida State in their 10th game of the regular season, only to fall to Boston College a week later in Notre Dame Stadium on a field goal as time expired.

* consensus national championship seasons
All poll references are to Associated Press poll.

100 The International Versions

Irish Go Overseas

When you think about Notre Dame football road trips, the normal inclination is to ponder Irish visits to Michigan Stadium (which seats 100,000+) to tackle the Wolverines or to the historic Los Angeles Coliseum to battle USC.

But don't forget about the international flair that the Irish have exhibited:

- The Notre Dame freshman football team played in Mexico City, Mexico, in 1971.
- The Irish defeated Miami 40–15 in the Mirage Bowl (the regular-season finale that year) at National Olympic Stadium in Tokyo, Japan, on Nov, 24, 1979. Vagas Ferguson carried 35 times for 177 yards and three touchdowns.
- No. 19 Notre Dame defeated Navy 54–27 at Croke Park in Dublin, Ireland, in a regular-season game played November 2, 1996, behind Autry Denson's 123 rushing yards and two touchdowns.
- An Irish alumni team won 14–10 against the Hamburg Blue Devils at Volksparkstadion in Hamburg, Germany, on July 8, 2000, thanks to an end-zone interception by Ivory Covington on the final play of the game.

At press time, former Notre Dame head coach Lou Holtz was slated to lead the Fighting Irish Legends, an alumni team made up of former Fighting Irish football players, for the Notre Dame Japan

Bowl 2009—to be played at the 55,000-seat Tokyo Dome in Japan's capital city on July 25, 2009. The game against the Japanese national team was to be the highlight of an eight-day visit to Tokyo to celebrate the 75th anniversary of the Japan American Football Association (JAFA).

Acknowledgments

Fortunately, there is no shortage of written material on the subject of Notre Dame football. In fact, check out item No. 94 in this book itself for a compendium of interesting titles relative to the Fighting Irish. However, one other "book" remained a huge resource.

Back in Notre Dame's 1977 national championship season, the *Notre Dame Football Guide* stood at a rather typical 96 pages for its 8½" x 11" format. As those team-produced media guides grew in size and scope, the Notre Dame version grew, as well. With a treasure trove of history at our fingertips, we researched anything and everything we could think of—and added liberally to the guide. We added detailed information on polls and national championship selections (in fact, the NCAA ultimately borrowed a tremendous amount of research that appeared on that subject in Dan Jenkins' book *Saturday's America*). By 2003, the guide grew to 484 pages—but prior to the 2005 season, the NCAA established a 208-page limit, leaving lots of material on the cutting-room floor.

A share of that copy became the raw material for a number of entries in this work—with original writing having come from a variety of individuals from the sports information staff, including myself, Karen Croake, Eddie White, Jim Daves, Mike Enright, Rose Pietrzak, Lisa Nelson, Doug Walker, Bernie Cafarelli, Brian Hardin, Michael Bertsch, Willie Shearer, Jeff Spelman, and others whose media guide contributions never listed specific authorship.

A special thanks to former staffer Pete LaFleur whose personal research and especially detailed analysis often lent particular perspective to subjects in and around Notre Dame athletics. Another special thanks to Carol Copley for all of her photo research and assistance.

Bibliography

A number of other works served as source material:

ABC Sports College Football All-Time All-America Team. Hyperion, 2000.

Bonifer, Michael, and Weaver, L.G. *Out of Bounds: An Anecdotal History of Notre Dame Football.* Piper Publishing, Inc., 1978.

Boyles, Bob, and Guido, Paul. *Fifty Years of College Football: A Modern History of America's Most Colorful Sport.* Sideline Communications, Inc., 2005.

Donovan, Jim; Marder, Keith; and Spellen, Mark. *The Notre Dame Football Encyclopedia.* Citadel Press, 2001.

Gullifor, Paul F. *The Fighting Irish on the Air: The History of Notre Dame Football Broadcasting.* Diamond Communications, Inc., 2001.

Layden, Joe. *Notre Dame Football A to Z.* Taylor Publishing, 1997.

MacCambridge, Michael. *ESPN College Football Encyclopedia.* ESPN Books, 2005.

Official 2008 NCAA Division I Football Records Book. NCAA, 2008.

Sterling, Mary Beth. *Look Out for the Manhole Cover.* Wagner/Mark Publishing, 1993.

The College Football Book. Sports Illustrated Books, 2008.

The College Game. Bobbs-Merrill, 1974.

Whittingham, Richard. *Saturday Afternoon.* Workman Publishing, 1985.